Personal&Social Education
and cross-curricular themes

Year 11

edited by

Jackie Hill • Jill Tordoff • Cathy Rushforth

Published by Evans Brothers Limited
2A Portman Mansions
Chiltern Street
London W1M 1LE

© copyright in the text Burnage High School and Manchester City Education Committee 1994
© copyright illustrations Evans Brothers Limited 1994

Designed by Can Do Design, Buckingham

First published 1994

Reprinted in 1996, 1998, 2000
Printed in Hong Kong by Dah Hua Printing

ISBN 0 237 51495 8

British Library Cataloguing in Publication Data.
A catalogue record for this book is available from the British Library.

Acknowledgements

This course was planned, written, trialled and evaluated by members of the staff of Burnage High School and advisory teachers from the Central District of Manchester's Education Development Service. Like any new course its success depended upon good teamwork, the experience of the team members and a great deal of time and effort. The authors would like to thank the other team members, listed below for their experience, professionalism and enthusiasm.

Ged Lee   Vic Johnson
Jenny Gow   Irene Birds
Ian Hope   Paul Pardy
John Jackson   Joan Collins
Paul Maxfield

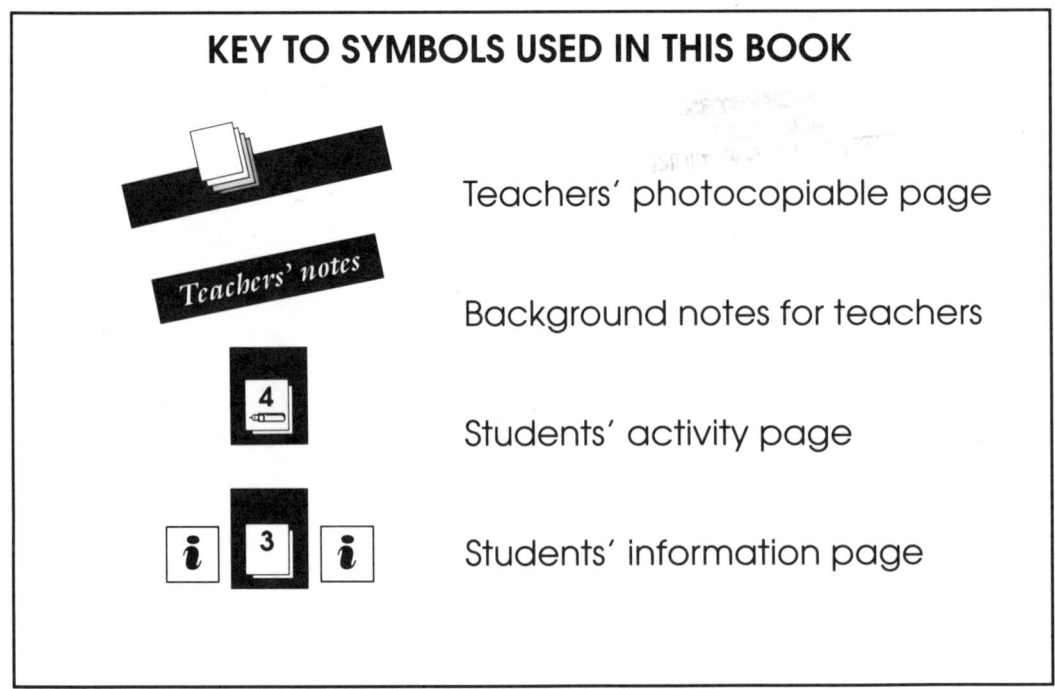

KEY TO SYMBOLS USED IN THIS BOOK

Teachers' photocopiable page

Background notes for teachers

Students' activity page

Students' information page

Personal & Social Education
and cross-curricular themes
Year 11

Contents

Term 2

Introduction

The importance of a PSE programme

Prior to the introduction of the National Curriculum most teachers had recognised that a number of issues crucial to the development of young people did not fall neatly into the curriculum of the Secondary School. However the material available at the time seemed to be very narrow in its content, and didactic in its delivery. This left many schools struggling with this area in an ad hoc way.

Recognition of the importance, not only of ensuring that all students had some knowledge and skills in these areas, but also of introducing them in a systematic way was encapsulated in the Education Reform Act. The act stated that all students should receive a broad and balanced curriculum which prepared them for adult life. The act also required schools to cover areas such as citizenship, health education, careers etc as part of the Cross-Curricular Themes, Skills and Dimensions.

A PSE programme will raise students' confidence, and help them to develop inter-personal skills, social skills and communication skills, all of which are vital in preparing students for adult life. It should be relevant to students' needs, and take into account the society in which they live. The programme should underpin the school pastoral system and offer support for school aims, especially regarding staff and student relationships and student inter-relationships. By highlighting areas such as bullying it should help to create a more open and supportive environment for all and provide valuable guidance for the future. The achievement of these aims will ensure that the school is a place where effective learning and the acquisition of skills can take place.

The development of the programme

Like many schools Burnage High School saw the need in 1986 to develop a coherent and comprehensive PSE programme for years 7 to 11. The teachers perceived a need for a comprehensive programme including the cross-curricular themes, which used a variety of teaching methodologies in order to engage students in it. They also wanted to offer a spiral curriculum, where students could revisit themes through years 7 to 11.

The school was successful in its bid for assistance from Manchester LEA to develop their materials. Central Manchester Education Development Service provided a team of advisory teachers who worked with the Burnage staff writing and trialling the material, using a team-teaching approach. The Education Development Service team also provided specific training in areas such as active learning approaches, drug education, sex education and health and healthy eating. The programme was trialled, revised and rewritten. This revision and updating has continued on all 7 to 11 course material.

The programme generated keen interest from other Manchester schools. A dissemination conference was held and secondary schools from Manchester and other local LEAs were given access to the programme.

Burnage High School is an inner-city multi-ethnic 11-18 boys' comprehensive. However, the programme has been trialled in various high schools to ensure that the materials are relevant and accessible to all students of secondary age.

The programme and how to use it

This is a broad and balanced programme which will interest and stimulate students and help to provide them with the guidance they need to be prepared for adult life.

The programme is based around the cross curricular themes of citizenship, environment, health, careers and economic and industrial awareness. Each theme has been divided into relevant strands, see below. Topics are then developed from these strands, see page 7. The themes have been broken down into teaching modules which translate the aims of the theme into a relevant learning experience for the students. This also allows the teacher extra flexibility, as the module can be taught in any order. It is also possible to move modules from one year to another should there be an opportunity to capitalise on a need. For example, the Health and Welfare (sex education) module in year 11, would work very well with some of the year 10 modules if the teacher believed it was appropriate.

Lesson plans for each module are designed to give teachers confidence when teaching the programme. The fact that few teachers consider themselves specialists in this area has been behind the structured framework of the programme. The materials can be delivered either by a specialist PSE team or through a team of form tutors. The year 10 book provides modules for a whole year's PSE work, the year 11 book provides modules for the two non-exam terms. The lessons are planned to last for an hour per week, although there is often more to do than time allows, particularly if students want to discuss elements of the module. Activities not covered in lessons can be completed outside the lesson, possibly as homework. This could help to involve parents into the programme.

The module

Each module has:

- A teacher introduction which outlines the objectives, methodology and resources needed.

- Lesson plans for each lesson in the module and any notes which may be applicable, and space for any individual notes to be recorded.

- Specific teacher information and/or teacher photocopiable sheets.

- *Student Booklet,* to be photocopied and given to each student at the beginning of the module. This contains all the materials they will need for the unit. Each booklet has its own cover and is designed to be a record of the unit, including self-evaluation. These should be retained by students for reference and to help when completing the National Record of Achievement in year 11.

THEMES AND STRANDS

CITIZENSHIP				
	1	Community variations	6	Similarities and differences
	2	Stability and change in communities	7	Experiences and opportunities
	3	Organisation, roles and laws	8	Custom and law
	4	Needs of individuals vs society	9	Fairness, justice and morals
	5	Cooperation and conflict		

ENVIRONMENT				
	1	Natural processes	7	The dependency of lives and livelihoods
	2	Impact of humanities	8	Conflicts
	3	Differences – past and present	9	Effects of past decisions and actions
	4	Issues: greenhouse effect etc.	10	Planning, design and aesthetics
	5	Legislature controls – policies & decision	11	Management and protection
	6	Interdependence of groups		

HEALTH				
	1	Effects of substances	6	Food and nutrition
	2	Sex education	7	Personal hygiene
	3	Family life education	8	Social, physical and economic factors
	4	Safety	9	Psychological aspects
	5	Health related exercise		

CAREERS				
	1	Self's strengths and weaknesses	6	Sectors of employment / job families
	2	Planning	7	Patterns and changes in employment
	3	Effective decision making	8	Opportunities and sources of information
	4	The role of work in self-development	9	Financial and legal elements
	5	Work related roles		

ECONOMIC/INDUSTRIAL AWARENESS				
	1	Key concepts	4	Consumers
	2	Creating wealth	5	Economy vs society
	3	Organisation / relationships	6	Role of government and international organisations

Programme topics

Year	Citizenship	Environment	Health	Careers	Economic/ Industrial awareness
7	Bullying Relationships – family, friends etc Moral education Child protection	Community actions Drugs awareness Smoking	Healthy eating Dental care Personal care skills First aid Growing up	Recognising and recording achievement	Study skills Advertising/ pressure to consume
8	Equal opportunities Conflict situations Bullying Friends Peer group pressure Rules and responsibilities	Drugs awareness Personal issues Local issues Global issues Environmental dangers Animal exploitation	Safety First – Emergency First Aid Health and fitness Relaxation Body image Health risks	Assertiveness training Looking ahead: – letter writing – telephone skills – research skills – expanding horizons – interviewing an adult	Roles of people in the community Media awareness Consumer issues Development issues
9	Self-esteem Bullying Child protection Family relationships Electing a representative Conflict Managing behaviour Writing policies Gender stereotyping	Drugs awareness and alcohol issues Respecting people and their environment	Personal hygiene Girls' and boys' relationships Being a teenager Religious and moral views of relationships	Body language Equal opportunities: – gender – race – the elderly – acceptable lifestyles – self-evaluation	Media pressures Community role play Advertising and sponsorship
10	Prejudice Political education You and the law Equal opportunities policies	Leisure Improving school environment	AIDS/HIV awareness Parenthood Family	Assessing and developing skills Interview techniques Self-evaluation Target-setting	Study skills/time management Work experience
11	A time to reflect	Working environment	Stress and relaxation Drugs and health Going to the doctor Alternative treatments Contraception STDs Sex education	Career opportunities and the job market Careers service and job centres National record of achievement C.V. Job and college applications Post-16 options	Economic patterns Developing employment trends in Britain and EU Work and paying taxes

Evaluation

In the past, Personal and Social Education (PSE) has been regarded as a'Cinderella' subject, even in a free period! However the value of PSE is now recognised and its place in the curriculum is assured. In order to consolidate its status and to ensure its relevance to students any PSE programme must have an evaluation process.

Throughout this programme, in years 7 to 10, there has been an inbuilt evaluation programme. At the end of each module there has been a *self-evaluation* sheet for students and teachers. At the end of each term there has been a *For the record* sheet for students. These sheets should have helped students to evaluate their work, their understanding of the module and to have highlighted areas still requiring information. They will also have provided teachers with a tool to evaluate the programme and its relevance to students, as well as a tool with which to monitor students.

The skills and information recorded on the evaluation sheets up to year 10 will be invaluable to students and teachers in completing the National Record of Achievement required of all students in year 11. There is also an evaluation module in the year 11 programme, *Time to reflect*. This aims to allow students time to reflect, before they have to complete their National Record of Achievement.

Group work strategies

These are useful groupwork strategies most of which are referred to throughout the programme. They can be used as directed and/or at any time, as appropriate.

Brainstorming

This means making a list of related ideas without thinking carefully about what springs to mind. Everything that participants shout out is recorded without discussion. No ideas are rejected. A brainstorming exercise should be spontaneous and brief. Some advantages of the technique are:

- all ideas are acceptable
- everybody is equal and has a contribution to make
- encourages imagination and creativity
- a quick way of generating a lot of information
- can help the group leader to assess the level of understanding
- is cooperative and open-minded
- can help with problem-solving
- helps to develop self-confidence

Ranking

This means listing a series of statements, pictures or objects according to the demands of the task, eg ranking a series of statements from agreement to disagreement, ranking a series of photographs from the most to the least stereotypical images. It is important to have each statement or picture on a separate sheet of card or paper so that they can be manoeuvred during discussion. Items can be ranked in order, or 'diamond ranked' using nine pieces of paper (see illustration). The latter is useful with, for example, value statements where it may not be possible to create a strict hierarchy.

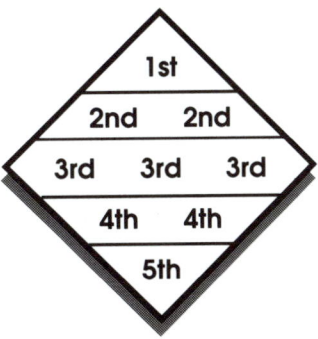

Photographs

There are many ways in which photographs can be used, eg to help create a story, to inform a role play, to provide discussion stimulus, to exemplify issues such as media bias, to break down stereotypes, to reinforce additional information or to offer a variety from the written form.

Snowballing

This is a way of sharing information and ensuring that everybody participates. Snowballing can take different forms, for example a topic can be introduced, considered individually then shared between pairs, fours, eights etc. This process can be stopped after any stage of sharing.

Values continuum

This is where individuals consider where they stand on particular issues and then rank themselves physically, in line. (It can also be done using appropriate statements on pieces of paper – see 'Ranking' – but the act of taking a 'standpoint' may be more thought-provoking or committed, eg:

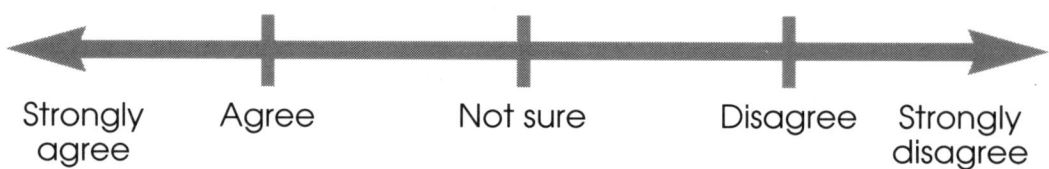

Strongly agree　　Agree　　Not sure　　Disagree　　Strongly disagree

Having established their relative viewpoints, students can be moved into structured discussion groups.

Role play

This is a way of allowing students to explore a situation (through the feelings and attitudes they might experience) by assuming the persona of a participant in a situation. Role play means presenting a set of attitudes rather than any physical change or characterisation. It is a way in which teachers can give students quick access to a topic or generate more concern for an issue. This can take place in smaller groups, possibly followed by a reporting back session, but it can also be an excellent medium for whole-group activities where the outcome need not be anticipated in advance. Role play can help individuals to share emotions or concerns which they feel unable to express normally since it allows students to say how they feel and at the same time distance themselves from the emotions by putting themselves in a fictional situation.

Ways of grouping students

Random Groups

- Birthdays eg 'everybody born in September'
- Attaching yourself to a set of descriptions eg 'everybody who supports Man City; everybody who supports Man United'
- Attaching numbers eg count 1, 2, 3, 4, 5, then group all the ones, all the twos etc
- Home numbers
- Alphabetical name order
- Class list (register order)
- Table groups
- Friendship groups
- Consciously mixed ability groups
- Team leaders picking teams – leaders may select more for competitive performance than when forming friendship groups
- Consciously mixed culture groups

Advantages and disadvantages of different types of groups

Teacher-selected groups:
- can create different/new groupings
- can break up friendship groups
- includes isolates
- can create classroom ethos
- can develop/encourage social skills
- can act as an icebreaker
- can result in 'ineffective' groups
- can facilitate mixed-ability work
- can support/enhance teacher 'control'
- can be quick.

Student-selected groups:
- can be exclusive
- can create hierarchies
- helps create a 'safe' working environment for individuals
- can help with bonding of groups
- can be used competitively
- can limit integration.

Summing up my achievements

Objectives

To provide students with the opportunity:

1 to reflect on and identify achievements in and out of school

2 to draft, write and edit a personal statement for their summative *Record of Achievement*

3 to practise speaking about their achievements to a range of people

4 to raise confidence.

Methodology

Lesson 1 After lesson introduction students may refer back to Year 10 modules to help in their discussions of personal qualities, also using a sheet from the *student booklet* as a prompt. In groups students discuss and complete the activity in the *student booklet*.

Lesson 2 Students draft their personal statements and review and check them with others. The statements should then be edited and word processed. Students may complete a curriculum vitae.

Lesson 3 Students practise talking about themselves and become fluent in presenting their personal statements in a range of situations.

Resources

Writing the tutor's section	16
Examples of personal statements	17
Student Booklet (1 per student)	21
Work from year 10 modules	
National Record of Achievement	
Dictionaries	
Word processing facilities	

Summing up my achievements

Lesson 1
The real you

1 Explain that students are going to look at their personal qualities. Remind the class of previous occasions when they have done this. They may care to use some of that work from the year 10.

2 Explain that personal qualities are important. We all have different ones. Which personal qualities are important and which ones do other people need to know about if they are going to make the best of you, eg employers, college lecturers, etc.

- Who is the real you?
- What makes you special?
- What have you got going for you?

3 Students discuss this issue using *student booklet* page 1. Get students to talk about this issue for themselves, using *The real you* as a prompt.

Either

a Put a student in the 'hot seat', ie put him or her in the centre of the group and fire the questions at him/her.

Or

b Ask students in pairs to take turns putting each other on the spot, using the questions for ideas. Stress importance of being positive about oneself.

4 Introduce the idea of a personal statement. Ask students to read *student booklet* page 2 which gives employers' and college lecturers' statements about how they appreciate and use these statements. Photocopy examples of personal statements on pages 17 and 18 for groups to read and decide which are the best and why. These are real examples, with the names changed. You might also like to photocopy and give students the examples from the National Record of Achievement on pages 19 and 20. Groups devise a list of things to include and not to include in a personal statement.

Students then complete *student booklet* page 3.

Lesson 2
Writing about yourself

1 After recapping on the last lesson individuals decide and note down what factual information about themselves they wish to include in a personal statement and what personal qualities they wish to mention. Use *student booklet* pages 4-6 as a prompt. Students should consider what evidence they have or need to back up what they say. Perhaps they could refer to their portfolios or the *self-evaluation* and *For the record* pages from the year 10 modules.

2 Students write first draft. Obviously this may take much longer than one lesson. Perhaps other opportunities can be created for them to draft and review work. Do students with special needs need other aids to do this, eg tape recorders or computers? Do any students need translation facilities?

Stress importance of sentences and paragraphs, spelling and punctuation.

Some examples of personal statements are included on pages 19-20. These could individually be photocopied on to the Personal Statement page of the National Record of Achievement. Once on this page it will be obvious that statements from Persons A, B, C and D are unacceptable, also they will look very sparse on the page, whereas the statements from Persons E and F are what is required.

3 Students review their work by using some of the following strategies. This does not all have to take place in class.

  • Read drafts, check using the dos and don'ts checklist from the previous lesson.
  • Read it to a partner and jointly edit it.
  • Show it to the tutor and discuss and edit it.
  • Show it to a parent or someone who knows them well and discuss whether it gives a true flavour of themselves.
  • Type it on a word processor and use the spellchecker.

4 Students write final draft. If possible this should be photocopied and taken home for discussion.

5 Final statement is typed on a word processor. Students may create a curriculum vitae if desired. Suggestions for inclusion in a CV are included on *student booklet* page 7.

Lesson 3
Talking about yourself

1 School and tutor arrange for students to practise talking about themselves, expanding upon their personal statements and becoming more fluent in describing their personal qualities and achievements. This practice can take place in a range of cross-curricular contexts, for example:

  • as part of a review with the tutor, eg 'I see from your Personal Statement that you . . . Can you tell me more about this?'
  • the focus of a discussion with the Careers Officer
  • groups role-play interviews
  • an oral component of GCSE English
  • individuals or groups practise speaking into a tape recorder, or in front of a video recorder
  • individuals take their personal statement to senior staff to discuss it.

NOTES
A briefing to help you complete the tutors section of the National Record of Achievement is on page 16.

Writing the tutor's section

General reminders

1 The section you write on the new National Record of Achievements is called **Other Achievements and Experiences.** It has to be negotiated between you and the student, probably at a review session.

The *Personal Statement* is the student's responsibility.

The *Curriculum Vitae* is the student's responsibility.

The *Personal Details* sheet is the student's responsibility.

The *Qualifications and Credits* sheet is filled in by the student after receiving his/her examination results.

The *Employment History* sheet is to be included in the Record of Achievement but is for the students to complete after they leave.

2 Be positive.

Don't worry that employers may be getting a rosy picture. They will read between the lines and notice your omissions. Avoid comments such as 'Could do better', 'Satisfactory' etc. If they could do better, say how or what they need to do.

3 If stuck, have you included the following:

- academic achievement, especially in the core skills
- communication skills
- problem-solving skills
- personal skills
- numeracy
- information technology
- modern language competence: remember to give credit to language/s spoken at home
- extra-curricular achievement
- personal interests
- home/school/community responsibilities
- personal qualities
- relationships with adults and peers
- work experience
- attendance/punctuality

4 Some young people may need an advocacy approach. If help is given, eg to a student with special needs, give the information in such a way as to identify these needs. Students could describe their achievements to a third party who would help them to write this up, or to annotate pictures and photographs if more appropriate.

Some examples

1   John is a pleasant and sociable student. He enjoys good relationships with his friends and gets on well with other students. He has an easy-going approach to life, but at the same time has a responsible attitude to school life and work. He takes care with his appearance and his attendance is good.

John generally works well and shows particular interest in practical subjects. He is able to assess his own ability and to work towards the targets he sets himself.

John has been a keen member of the school football team since Year Seven and also plays out of school. He also enjoys socialising.

2   Sharon is a very pleasant and cooperative student who has a positive and cheerful approach to school life and work. She socialises well with close friends and others and displays particularly good inter-personal skills. She has a sympathetic and understanding nature and is thoughtful and caring in her dealings with others. Sharon relates well to members of staff and is able to discuss feelings and issues with them without any loss of politeness or good manners.

Sharon is a conscientious worker who always gives of her best. She is able to assess her own weaknesses and take any necessary action to rectify problems. She has given some thought to her future and knows what targets she must set in order to achieve her ambitions. She has the determination and ability to achieve her goals.

Sharon takes care with her appearance. Attendance and punctuality have been excellent throughout her school career.

3   Daniel is an extremely pleasant, polite and friendly individual. He has a mature outlook and is an asset to the school.

Daniel works well as part of a group. There are many examples of his ability to cooperate with others. He has taken part in the Duke of Edinburgh Award Scheme and is about to receive his Silver Award. As part of his involvement in the Award Scheme, Daniel has gone on several expeditions. On these he has demonstrated his determination and his ability to make positive contributions to the work of a team.

Daniel is extremely reliable. He has attended school regularly and is always punctual. He has a keen interest in music and plays the trombone in several orchestras and bands. Daniel is a prominent member of the school's orchestra. He has set an excellent example to younger players by his regular attendance at rehearsals and concerts.

Daniel is keen on amateur radio. He is a member of the Radio Society of Great Britain and the Anglesey C.B. 'DX' Club. His interest in radio demonstrates his ability to understand technical issues and to adopt a positive and committed approach to his interests.

Daniel is keen to follow a career in graphic design. He likes art and paints at home. In school he has studied photography as part of his extension studies programme. Also he has given up his own time after school to follow his interest in photography.

Daniel is an able and conscientious young man. He is keen to do well and has an active approach to life. I am sure that he will make a success of whatever he decides to do in the future.

4   Faisal might be considered by some to be a model student. His attendance and punctuality record is excellent. His attitude to the academic requirements of school life is also excellent. He has completed all his GCSE coursework ahead of time, the quality of his work being of a very high standard.

Faisal is a good all-rounder and has strengths in all areas of the curriculum. He has the academic discipline required to learn a modern language, French, achieving an A grade in the mock examinations. He is orally fluent in Urdu and can read Arabic. He has also shown he can work accurately and imaginatively to solve problems, as witnessed by his high quality CDT Realisation projects: a wooden drawing board, a clock complete with electronic movement and a coffee/games table.

Faisal is well liked by both staff and students, the latter choosing him as their representative on the year and school council, a body which presents students' ideas to the school's management. He obviously communicates well with all members of the school community. He has made good use of his time in school both in normal curriculum time and also out of school, being a valued and skilful member of the soccer team and also giving up his own time to re-furbish and re-decorate the school's Outdoor Pursuits Centre.

He has achieved unit credits in soccer, French and Science. Faisal is a keen model maker; he uses construction kits to make his models, usually aircraft, and then paints them to make them as accurate as possible.

In October he spent two weeks on Work Experience with British Gas from whom he gained an excellent reference. He completed a variety of tasks from updating computer records to assisting a service engineer in the repair and maintenance of domestic central heating boilers.

At the present time, Faisal has no clear ambitions, but he would be equally at home either in the field of further education or the world of work. He has taken the advice offered and left his options open. Whatever Faisal decides for the future, I can without reservation assure you that this student will give 100% of his abilities.

Personal statements

Person A

I am a student at . . . . School. I am going to do my GCSE's soon. I want to be a vet.

Person B

I am really good at working with people. I am very helpful and reliable. I like playing records and going out.

Person C

I am studying French, English, Science, Geography, Maths and Home Economics at GCSE. I like Science best. I help in the library at dinner time. I want to go to College and then to University to study Chemical Engineering. I am a member of the School Council.

Person D

I have never been good at anything since I came here. None of the other people like me. The teachers all pick on me. I have held no positions of responsibility. All the subjects are boring but particularly French. I don't really care what job I get as long as it's well paid.

Person E

I am a person who can make friends easily and enjoy the company of both male and female friends. People say that I am warm and sensitive. I like to think that I can help anybody who needs help, and always, no matter what the situation, remember that there is always someone worse off than me. I like to be with people who can take things seriously when necessary but know when and how to have fun, like myself. I enjoy being in a crowd of friends but realise that private and personal time is essential to me. I believe that family life is very important and enjoy being part of a big, happy and loving family. I really enjoy my life but take every day as it comes. I have a very determined and ambitious personality. I don't believe in planning the future although I do have ambitions and dreams.

At the moment I am working towards my GCSE's which I will be taking in the summer. I believe I have worked to the best of my ability in my subjects. I am very interested in the creative department. I really enjoy Art, I feel it is very relaxing and fulfilling. My favourite subjects are Art, English and Business Studies. I have, so far, enjoyed my life at school. I have made many friends with students and staff. I hope to be successful in my exams and then go on to college.

I have enjoyed playing the clarinet in which I achieved up to grade four, distinction. I also played the guitar and enjoyed singing in different choirs. I really enjoyed organising several school discos for which all profits raised went to St Mary's Babycare Unit. I enjoyed the creative side of my subjects and even though I am not taking Art A Level, I will continue with it in my spare time to relax and unwind. I have enjoyed being in the friendly, warm community of the school and have not only worked hard, but had a lot of fun too.

I have no settled ambitions except to be successful in anything that I do, now or in the future.

© Burnage High School and Manchester City Education Committee

Person F

I have been a student at this school for five years and at present I am studying for my GCSE exams. I am being entered for 8 GCSEs. These are: English Language, English Literature, Science (2 GCSEs), French, Geography, Maths and Art and Design, as this and other art-related subjects are what I wish to study up to degree level when I leave in July 1991. I am hoping to be accepted for a place in a Sixth Form College, as I wish to study A levels in Art, Art and Design, and Photography in September. I enjoy French and Geography too, and these subjects may be useful to me later on in my career. My mock examination results were good for French and Geography. I achieved 74% overall in both Geography papers. The Geography coursework accounts for 25% too, and this was not included in the mock exam grade, so in the actual GCSE exams it will bring up my final grade.

I enjoy participating in extra-curricular activities, non-GCSE and other activities such as photography, amateur radio and playing my trombone in seven bands/orchestras and two groups out of school. I enjoy black and white photography too. I have constructed my own darkroom using the available loftspace in our house. I am involved in the Duke of Edinburgh's Award Scheme and have passed my Bronze and Silver Awards. I am currently undergoing my training for the Gold Award through the school. I have passed my First Aid Certificate, my Bronze, Silver and Gold Awards for swimming (ASA/ASSA), and I have passed my Associated Board exams for the trombone, grades three and four with distinction and grade five with merit. I play tenor and bass trombone in the local area band/orchestras.

I also play squash regularly, although I only play for pleasure and exercise, I am not a member of any teams or clubs as yet. I am a member of the Incorporated Society for Amateur Radio Enthusiasts, the Radio Society of Great Britain, and I am working towards some awards associated with amateur radio.

I am applying to be accepted for a place in a Sixth Form College and I should be going for several interviews in April and May. I have had to single out specific colleges that cater for my A level needs such as photography.

P**ersonal** & S**ocial** E**ducation**

and cross-curricular themes

Student Booklet

Term 1 Module 1

S**umming up my achievements**

name

form   date

The real you

Ask your partner these questions. Don't give him/her too much time to answer, then change places

What do you most like about yourself?

What do other people like about you?

If you had £1 million, what would you do with it?

What do you most worry about?

What things make you laugh?

What is the best thing you have done in your life so far?

If you were a character from history, who would it be? Why?

What qualities in yourself do you most admire?

What qualities in a person do you most admire?

In 5 years time, where do you see yourself? What will you be doing?

The real you • continued •

What employers and colleges say about the personal statement

I like the personal statement to be refreshingly honest.

The student's personal statement is a very good document, the first thing I always read.

There are some excellent examples where the school has allowed the students the freedom to decide what achievements to include. Students must be encouraged to analyse themselves and present a very personal picture. Statements must be honest and relate to the young person concerned, not a general statement which could relate to anyone.

I wish I had had something like this when I left school.

Students should bring their Record of Achievement to interviews and be prepared to talk proudly about the things that are in it.

I like to see evidence of the whole person, what are their aspirations and ambitions in life?

I want to know about how the student approaches the subjects generally. This shows us what the student can actually do, what he/she has done so far, what their future goals are and what actions they intend to take in order to meet those goals.

The Record of Achievement is not only important in the interview, but also when the person is at college, university, training or in employment. It should form the basis of personal record-keeping for life.

Make the most of your chance to show these people what you are really about!

Writing about yourself in a personal statement

There are some personal statements on page 23. Personal statements are meant to give other people a good idea of your qualities as a person. Read them and comment on each of them for good and bad points.

Which personal statements were good/bad?

Why?

Do you agree that the good ones are good because the writers have included certain statements which give a good *flavour* of their personalities and strengths?

Now think of a list of do's and don'ts for writing a personal statement.

Do's	Don'ts

Cartoons

Do any of these cartoons remind you of yourself? Think about which of your personal qualities you would like to write about in your personal statement.

You enjoy being with other people. You get on quickly with people when you first meet. You work well in a group, where you cooperate with others to carry out a task. Groups you are in work well together because you encourage everyone to do their bit and take pride in the end result.

If you say you will do something you will do it. You can be relied upon to start on time, keep to deadlines and do the best job you possibly can.

You have a good record of punctuality and attendance.

You are good at thinking up your own new ideas and don't copy other people. You are original and creative.

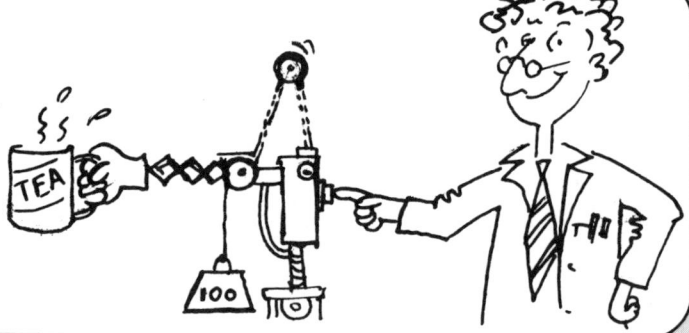

You take on new things with energy and enthusiasm.

You take care over the things you do and make sure you get them right.

before

You can sort things out for yourself. You don't expect others to show or help you. You are independent and resourceful.

...after

You have a good sense of dress and you make sure your appearance is suitable for the occasion.

You have a lot of common sense. You are mature for your age and tend to act responsibly, thinking ahead and considering the consequences of your actions.

You are good at concentrating on a problem and seeing it through to the end. You don't give up when the going gets tough.

You listen to, understand and sympathise with other people. You think about their needs and help them where you can.

You are organised. You plan ahead, get what you need and sort out what you are going to do.

Curriculum Vitae

What should go in your Curriculum Vitae?

Name

Date of Birth

Address and Telephone number

- **Secondary Education:**   Name of School/s, address of school/s, date/s attended

- **Qualifications:**   Examination results, subjects, level eg GCSE grades
Other qualifications eg First Aid Certificate, Unit Credits, Music certificates, life-saving badge, Duke of Edinburgh award

- **Experience:**   Positions of responsibility in school, community or at home
Extra-curricular interests eg sports, clubs, leisure interests

- **Work Experience:**   Name and Address of Employer, nature of placement
Any paid employment eg Saturday job, babysitting, etc

- **Referees:**   Usually one personal and one work or educational referee with their name, address, position and telephone number.

Careers

Objectives

To provide students with the opportunity:

1. to research information on the changing nature of the job market and anticipate likely opportunities
2. to familiarise themselves with looking through the jobs section in local papers
3. to see what kinds of jobs are available in the local area
4. to interpret job advertisements
5. to focus on a particular place of work and the range of employment it offers
6. to consider the difference between specialist and transferable skills
7. to identify reliable sources of career information
8. to consider post-sixteen career paths
9. to plan a personal career path
10. to write job and/or college applications and covering letters
11. to practise effective questioning for information, eg via telephone skills
12. to consider some of the financial implications of employment.

Methodology

Lesson 1 After lesson introduction students discuss the questions posed and agree guidelines for their research. Groups research their area and report back to class. Students reflect on their own career objectives and list information they require and create an action plan.

Lesson 2 Students complete *student booklet* page 11 in groups with newspapers. After class feedback students complete *student booklet* in pairs. Students reflect on their action plan and make any necessary changes.

Lesson 3 Students think about where they are in terms of making a career choice. In groups, students discuss 'gender' exercise. Students should read information sheets on post-sixteen options and complete the activity in the *student booklet* in pairs. After reflection, students should again consider their action plan.

Lesson 4 Students study information on deadlines for education and training. Students receive self-study pack and practise those skills they require. In groups students practise their telephone skills.

Lesson 5 In pairs, students complete *student booklet* activity and report back to class. Students participate in a game which provides oral questioning practise.

Lesson 6 Students either individually or in pairs complete the activities in the *student booklet*. After feedback try to assess if students have understood the financial implications of their choice. Complete the lesson with the quiz.

Resources

Career Path sheets A and B (1 per group)	34
Job cards (1 set)	36
Student Booklet (1 per student)	39
Self-study packs	63
Copies of local evening paper	
Copies of free press newspaper	
Internal telephone and tape recorder	
Up-to-date information from DSS on Income Support rules for people under eighteen	

Careers

Lesson 1
What does the future hold?

1 Explain that careers aren't necessarily for life. Things in the world outside are changing fast. Some jobs which lots of people do now may disappear. Other jobs none of us have heard of will become necessary. We need to be flexible. We need to think ahead and make sure we have the skills that society will need. *Student booklet* pages 1-10 has information about five changes which will affect all of us in our working lives and at home. These sheets could be photocopied to A3 size and displayed in the classroom.

In groups, students should research one area. Students should pick out the main things which seem important to them. These should be discussed and guidelines agreed for the research.

2 Each group should research their area

3 Each group will then report to the class on what they have found out and how this may affect them in the future. This is followed by class discussion: What general skills and personal qualities make us valued by employers in the future?

4 Personal reflection. Ask students to think about their own possible career interests. Are they already sure? Do they need to find out more about different occupations? Do they need to think more about their own personal interests and abilities? Do they have accurate information about possible education and training?

The next few weeks are a chance to get their ideas and information sorted out because some decisions need to be made soon.

Students should jot down their ideas and the information they know they need on their sheet headed **Action plan** for this careers module. This action plan will be reviewed and revised throughout the module. Students then decide which items they can discuss with which people. Students write an agenda for discussions with different people and a checklist of targets they will have met by the end of the unit. Encourage students to start now.

Lesson 2
Job search: what's available?

1 Explain objectives 1 – 4.

2 Divide class into small groups of three to four and distribute a copy of a local evening paper and a free press newspaper to each group. You can use the advertisement on *student booklet* page 14 if necessary. Students complete *student booklet* page 11, *Job search: group task*. Circulate and provide help as required.

3 Groups report back answering the following questions:

- Which job category had the most jobs and which the least?
- Did all the groups have similar findings? If not, why not?
- Were there any surprises?
- What have we learnt about the availability of jobs in this area?
- Would the jobs section in other parts of the UK show a similar picture?
- Are there fewer unskilled and manufacturing jobs available?
- Are there more skilled and service jobs available?
- What will be the likely pattern for the future?

Offer input and extend the discussion.

4   Divide groups into pairs, Ask students to refer to and complete *student booklet* page 12 *Job search: pair tasks.* Circulate and provide help as required.

5   In conclusion, ask students to reflect on and amend their own action plan from last lesson.

Lesson 3
Decisions, decisions

1   Ask students to think about where they personally are up to in terms of deciding about their future direction.

Do they have a pretty clear idea?

Do they have some idea, say three or four occupations they could see themselves doing?

Do they have no idea?

This lesson will allow them to look at the possibilities for choosing a definite career path **or** for putting off their decision until later by choosing a general education at age sixteen.

2   Introduce **Career Paths**. Distribute sheets A and B to students in groups. Secretly make sure that half the students have sheet A and the other half have sheet B.

Groups read about the characters and predict their career paths. After group discussion, groups report back to the class. Then disclose to the class your trick. The only difference between Jack and Jackie was their sex. Did this make the students choose stereotyped career paths or not?

The moral of this story is: Keep your options open. Don't dismiss ideas out of hand. A non-stereotyped career might be just what would suit you!

3   Explain necessity of being clear about the options available post sixteen. To help them sort it out they should read through *student booklet* pages 14-17, *Made your mind up?*, *Glossary*, *Flow chart*, and *Case studies.*

Discuss and explain the sheets.

4   As a check that they have understood this information, ask pairs of students to use the information on the *case study* sheets to complete the *flow chart* activity. They should decide which route each character takes and draw a differently coloured line for each route.

5   Time for personal reflection. Ask each student to consider his or her own interests and aptitudes. The students draw their own personal flow diagram if they can or review their action plan and point out the advantages of talking to as many people as they can about the options. Accurate information is necessary.

6   Give students pep talk. Try to allay any anxieties students have about making decisions now. Decisions can always be changed. They may discover that it isn't what they really want, that there are no jobs in the field or that they and their interests have changed.

Career change is very likely in their lives. Their best bet is to make sure that education or training that they opt for now will be useful in a variety of situations. The training and education they get now should be transferable.

Lesson 4
Getting a place

1 Teacher gives students information on local deadlines for applications to post-sixteen education and training, for example:

YT Schemes
Sixth Forms, Sixth Form Colleges
Further Education
Local Employment

Liaise with your Head of Careers and Careers Officer.

2 Give each student a copy of the *self-study pack*. It is their responsibility to make sure they have had enough practice in writing covering letters and application forms. In the pack are examples of application forms. When necessary students should fill these in, get feedback from their tutor, amend them and give them to their tutor who will send them off. Feedback from local employers and the school careers officer is also very valuable.

3 Brief students on the importance of telephone skills. A skill everyone needs at this stage is the ability to ask for information. Using the telephone is often the quickest and most efficient way of doing this. Students work in groups to find out how good they are at asking for information over the telephone. Each student from the group, in turn, has to ring a mystery number. They should either arrange to visit a college to see someone about a course (eg BTEC First in Business and Finance, or a real one of their choice) or find out some details about what to do on the first day of their Work Experience.

4 Students prepare themselves, referring to *Telephone skills* sheet in the *self-study pack* for guidance. Students use internal telephone to ring the mystery number and ask for the relevant information. Tape the conversation. Other members of the group watch and grade their performance. Staff member or volunteer on the other end responds and makes notes so as to give honest feedback.

5 Students listen to themselves on tape and report back to their tutor, group and person on the other end of the phone.

Further practice and analysis.

Lesson 5
What's my line?

1 Explain objectives 5 and 6 and describe the range of jobs in a large institution such as a hospital and explain what transferable and specialist skills are.

2 Divide class into pairs and ask them to complete *student booklet* pages 18-19 *Job categories checklist*. Circulate and provide help as required.

3 Receive feedback from pairs:

• Were there any jobs difficult to categorise? Which?
• How many had transferable skills? Which type?

Stress the importance of having transferable skills in today's job market. As an example you could introduce the idea of a new employer, say the BBC, coming to interview the people working in the hospital. Each student should take the part on of one of the staff and explain how their skills could be relevant to the new employer.

4 Ask pairs to double up into groups of four. Distribute eight *What's my line?* cards to each. Explain how the game is played: one person is to do a simple mime of the job on the card and the others are to ask twenty questions which can be answered 'yes' or 'no'; each person can have two turns; if they exhaust the cards ask them to think of their own examples and continue the game.

Stress

- that the person 'on' must think carefully about what the job involves before answering the question
- that the rest of the group must try to develop effective questioning for information and work together to achieve this end.

5   In conclusion, ask students to refer back to their action plan. They should add to their sheet any occupations they wish to research.

Lesson 6
Work and pay

1   Explain objective 12.

2   Divide class into pairs. Ask students to complete *student booklet* page 20 *Work and pay – what do you know?* Circulate to provide help as necessary.

3   Receive feedback and answer any questions regarding these pages.

4   Ask students either individually or in pairs to complete *student booklet* page 22 *Work and pay – payslip.*

5   Provide answers to questions on this sheet.

6   Ask students to make sure they also understand the financial implications of the particular career path they are choosing post-sixteen.

7   To check on their financial understanding, students can test each other on *student booklet* page 23 or have a whole class quiz.

Career paths • A •

Form _____

Date _____

Read below about a person who, like you, is in Year 11. Decide what his future will be like by choosing a likely career path for him.

Jack Jones, aged 16 is:
- popular with both staff and students
- nice-looking and has a good sense of humour

He has just gained 6 GCSEs at grades C or above:

English Language
English Literature
Combined Science, 2 passes
Geography
Maths

He would like to work with people. He enjoys school but would like to start earning money as soon as possible.

Group task

Discuss what you know about Jack. Try to agree on Jack's future career path.

1   What will Jack do next? ....

....

2   At what age will he leave school? ....

3   At what age will he leave full-time education? ....

4   What do you think Jack will be doing one year after leaving full-time education? ....

....

5   What is Jack's likely career path between now and when he is 30 years old? ....

....

....

Career paths · B ·

Form _____

Date _____

Read below about a person who, like you, is in Year 11. Decide what her future will be like by choosing a likely career path for her.

Jackie Jones, aged 16 is:
- popular with both staff and students
- nice-looking and has a good sense of humour

She has just gained 6 GCSEs at grades C or above:

English Language
English Literature
Combined Science, 2 passes
Geography
Maths

She would like to work with people. She enjoys school but would like to start earning money as soon as possible.

Group task

Discuss what you know about Jackie. Try to agree on Jackie's future career path.

1 What will Jackie do next? ....

....

2 At what age will she leave school? ....

3 At what age will she leave full-time education? ....

4 What do you think Jackie will be doing one year after leaving full-time education? ....

....

5 What is Jackie's likely career path between now and when she is 30 years old? ....

....

....

Job cards • What's my line? •

STREET PERFORMER	TOUR GUIDE	ACTOR
TEACHER	SPORTS COACH (think of the sport)	MUSICIAN (think of the instrument)
SOCIAL WORKER	NANNY	SURGEON
DENTIST	DOCTOR	COMPUTER PROGRAMMER
NURSE	ARCHITECT	BILL POSTER
TRUCK DRIVER	SECURITY GUARD	CHECK-OUT OPERATOR

Job cards • **What's my line?** •

VICAR/PRIEST/ IMAM/RABBI (choose one)	POLICEMAN	ELECTRICIAN
LIBRARIAN	PARKING METER ATTENDANT	SELL SHARES ON THE STOCK MARKET
WINDOW DRESSER	FASHION MODEL	RECEPTIONIST
SHOPKEEPER	SOLDIER	PACKER
PORTER	CROUPIER	ASTRONAUT
OPERA SINGER	BARRISTER	POLITICIAN

Job cards What's my line?

REFUSE DISPOSAL OPERATIVE	PEST CONTROL OFFICER	TRANSLATOR
TV CAMERA OPERATIVE	GRAPHIC DESIGNER	SURVEYOR
RADIO BROADCASTER	DISC JOCKEY	LIFT OPERATOR
SHOPKEEPER	SCAFFOLDER	FIRE PERSON
PUBLIC RELATIONS OFFICER	BUTCHER	WATCH REPAIRER
PERSONNEL OFFICER	NEWSPAPER REPORTER	AIRLINE PILOT

Personal & Social Education
and cross-curricular themes

Student Booklet

Term 1 Module 2

Careers

name

form   date

EUROPE HERE WE COME!
or goodbye Great Britain?

Just how ready are we for the changes that are waiting just around the corner with the changes in Europe during the 1990s and beyond?

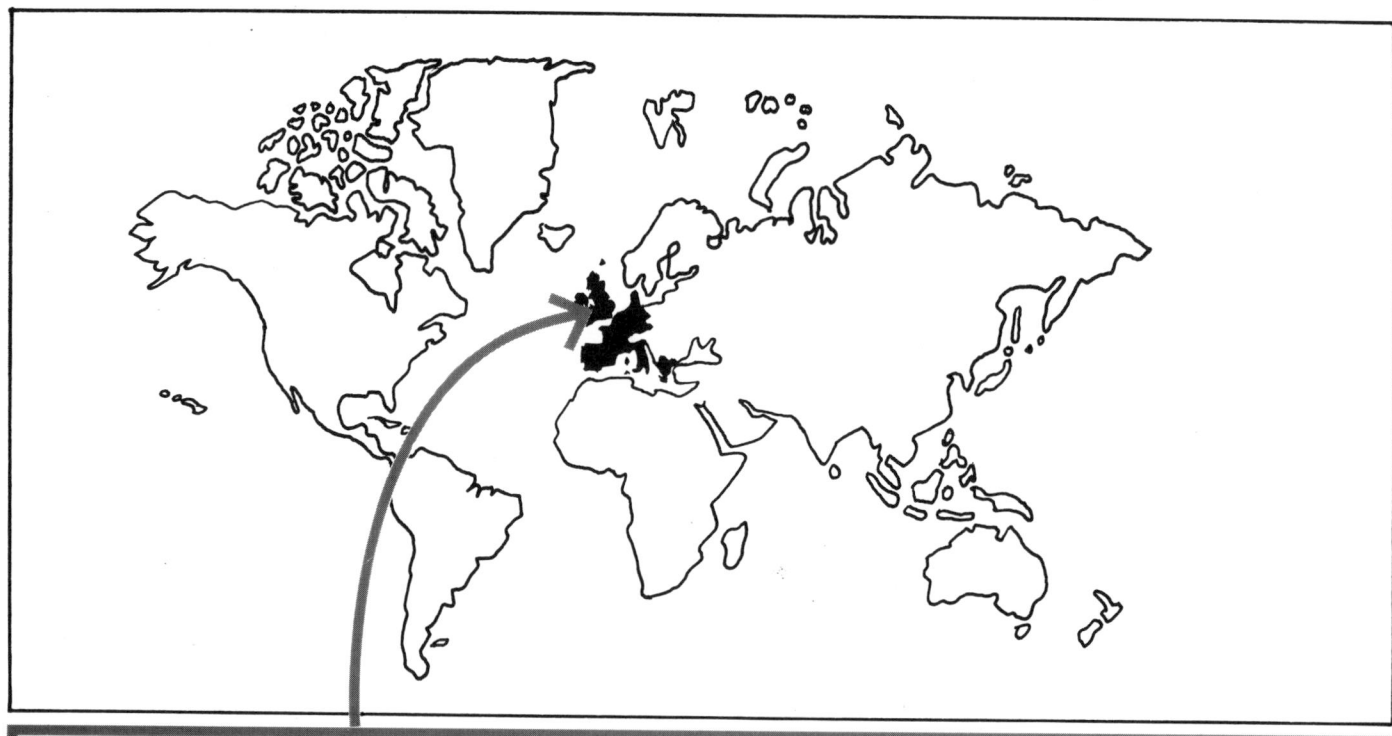

There are 15 countries in the European Union that form a single market:

Austria	Britain	Belgium	Denmark
Finland	France	Greece	Ireland
Italy	Luxembourg	Netherlands	Portugal
Spain	Sweden	West Germany	

Although the European Union does not look very large on the world map, it is one of the three most powerful trading blocs along with the United States and Japan.

SO WHAT WILL THIS MEAN FOR US? . . .

What does the future hold? • Europe •

Benefits for Trade and Industry

- Goods will be able to travel freely across the frontiers of these countries, there will be no more time-wasting forms to fill in.
- British exporters will have a golden opportunity to get out into Europe and sell their goods and services.
- However, the Europeans will be trying just as hard to sell their goods here.
- If European-produced goods are cheaper because they pay lower wages, will British-produced goods lose out?

Will we lose our rights?

Changes in Europe may bring some improved legal and social rights for all EU Nationals.
Politicians in Europe are planning to:
- improve maternity and paternity leave
- safeguard against unfair dismissal
- ensure the right to join a trade union
- establish a minimum wage.

Opportunities - but can we take them?

In general we in Britain are very much behind when it comes to speaking other languages well. Most people in Europe speak much better English than we do German, Spanish, French, Greek, etc.
New laws on employment mean we can go wherever we want in Europe - if we can get someone to offer us a job.
- Who will want to employ us if we can't speak their language?
- Will we have to compete for jobs in Britain with well-qualified Europeans speaking fluent English?
- Those of us who are fluent in world languages such as Japanese, Urdu, Chinese and Swahili should find that there are increasing numbers of employers needing these skills.

Remember, all those people who have British passports will be known as EU Nationals and they will have the right to work anywhere in the European Union.

The 1990s will certainly bring changes and opportunities: try to make sure you are in touch with what is happening and that you benefit from them.

Houseperson's choice? Home before work?

Society as we know it is changing fast.

- Gone are the days when you could assume that a woman's place is in the home.
- Gone are the days when you could assume that a man saw his main aim in life as being the family breadwinner.
- Gone are the days when you could assume that people lived in families of mother, father and children. People live in all sorts of family arrangements, or even alone.

Surveys show that more of us, men and women, are wanting equal opportunities at home and at work.

People won't laugh at us if we say we want

- to spend time with our children when they are young and be able to care for them when they are ill.
- to plan our careers so that we can fit in both a rewarding home life and a working life that gives us job satisfaction.
- to have leisure time that will allow us to follow our individual interests.
- to develop our skills throughout our adult lives so that we have a chance to get on in our chosen field of work.

We want quality of life . . . but how do we get it?

What is holding us back?

- Some attitudes that we have don't help.
- Some things will have to change in society if we are going to get what we want out of life.

Sharing responsibilities

We all need to take responsibility for . . .

- caring for others, whether it is our own children and families, or the elderly or disabled who sometimes need our help. Whether we are men or women it is our business. Just as we need women in technical jobs, we need men in caring jobs.
- sharing jobs out fairly around the home, making sure we do our bit and don't lumber someone else with the time-consuming tasks that eat into leisure time.

Employers need to . . .

- consider all of us as having home responsibilities and allow us parental leave and sometimes flexible working hours.
- make it easier to start new jobs after having had a break from paid work.
- build in opportunities for further training and promotion whatever our age.
- not expect employees to be able to move around the country or between countries at the drop of a hat.
- consider providing good quality child-care and holiday schemes for school-age children.
- shake up their ideas and recruit men and women to non-traditional jobs.

Remember . . .

All of these things should apply equally to men and women regardless of race, colour, disability, marital status, sexual orientation or age.

The next few years will certainly bring changes and opportunities: make sure you are in touch with what is happening and that you protect your rights.

What does the future hold? · Demographic time bomb ·

Where have all the young ones gone?

The next few years will see a 'demographic time bomb' when changes in the population will make a big difference to our lives.

The number of eighteen-year-olds is going to fall dramatically during the mid-1990s.

Planners think we can expect to see:

- employers queuing up to snap up those 18 - 21 year olds they can recruit.

- plenty of vacant jobs in teaching, the armed forces and nursing professions which up till now have always relied on young people to fill their vacancies.

- employers looking to attract other recruits, eg women, ethnic minorities, mature people and returners to work. To do this they will have to offer:

  on-the-job training
  workplace nurseries or childcare vouchers
  parental leave and flexitime

- more jobs in the caring and health services to cope with the growing army of pensioners.

44

Grey power rules OK?

Is Britain facing an American-style crisis?

In the 1990s the number of people of retirement age, and especially the over 80s, is set to rise dramatically. Will the army of grey-haired pensioners be mobilised to use their votes to press politicians to give them 'grey rights'?

- the right to work
- bigger pensions and more benefits
- special facilities

And how will younger working people feel when they are asked to pay more taxes towards supporting increasing numbers of pensioners?

And there's more . . .

More old people means more hospitals will be needed; more home helps and more assistance for those still living at home; and more young families may have to consider how best to care for their aging parents and grandparents.

Up till now there have been plenty of young people in work whose taxes have paid the pensions of the over 60s. But the number of eighteen-year-olds is going to fall dramatically between now and the mid 1990s.

And don't they deserve it!

Many who have worked hard all their lives deserve the best care and support when they are least able to provide it for themselves. Won't you expect the same when you are old? All the same, we all need to plan for our own future and those of our elderly relations.

Computers take over!

Will Britain be left behind in the race for robots? . . .

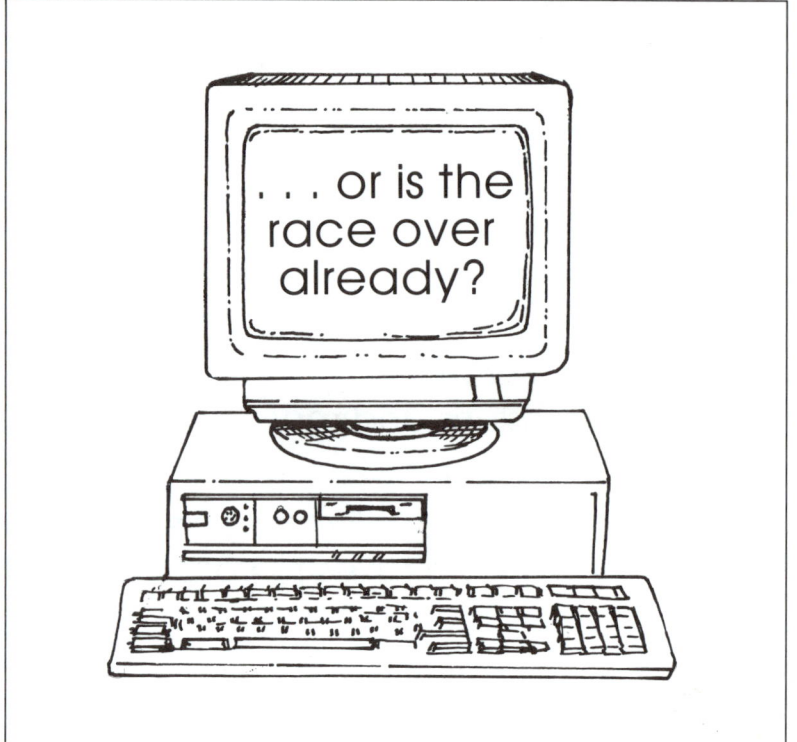

. . . or is the race over already?

The signs are that Britain is being left behind in the race to develop the use of computers in all aspects of our lives.

In comparison with our competitors in America and Japan:

- Britain is not producing enough computer scientists or systems analysts to fill the vacancies in our major companies.
- Those graduates who are produced are snapped up by American and other companies for plum jobs abroad.

And things are no better when it comes to more ordinary jobs.

- Many companies need all their employees to be able to type and operate word processors in the streamlined electronic offices of the future.
- As health service records are computerised doctors and nurses will have to key in to the new information technology skills.
- The police, local government agencies, shops and service industries are all going over to using computers to store records, make orders and keep accounts.
- Workers in many fields are using computers to help them design and manufacture their products.

Whatever your job, the chances are that you are going to have to learn to use a keyboard!

Some planners are even predicting that factories and offices could be the workplaces of the past. They say -

[handwritten: More or less power.]

- Manufacturing, such as cars, and engineering will be carried out mainly by robots. Just a few highly skilled workers will need to be on hand when things go wrong. *[handwritten: Factory of the future?]*
- There will be plenty of jobs available for those with computer skills and in training everyone to use the new information technology.
- There will be fewer jobs available in assembly type factory work, the robots will be doing that!
- People will be able to work from home, with their computer connected with a modem via their telephone to their firm or office's central computer.
- Some companies already use computers to do work for people in other countries. One in Ireland processes the records for a company in America - because it's cheaper and just as convenient.

This is the information technology revolution . . .

Make sure you are aware of what's going on and learn the necessary skills so that you won't be left behind or worse . . .

All the original worksheets and the lesson plans for this PSE programme were completed by teachers on the Apple Macintosh Computer and the final version to be sent to the printer was completed by graphic designers on the Apple Macintosh . . . this is called Desk Top Publishing.

What does the future hold? • Economic change •

The service revolution – the end of industry!

Signs that Britain is fast becoming a non-industrial nation are welcomed by some as evidence that the necessary economic changes are being made to take us to the year 2000.

But others paint a picture of gloom and say we won't be able to produce any high-tech or low-tech goods and that we will be reduced to depending on tourism and financial dealing to earn our living as a nation.

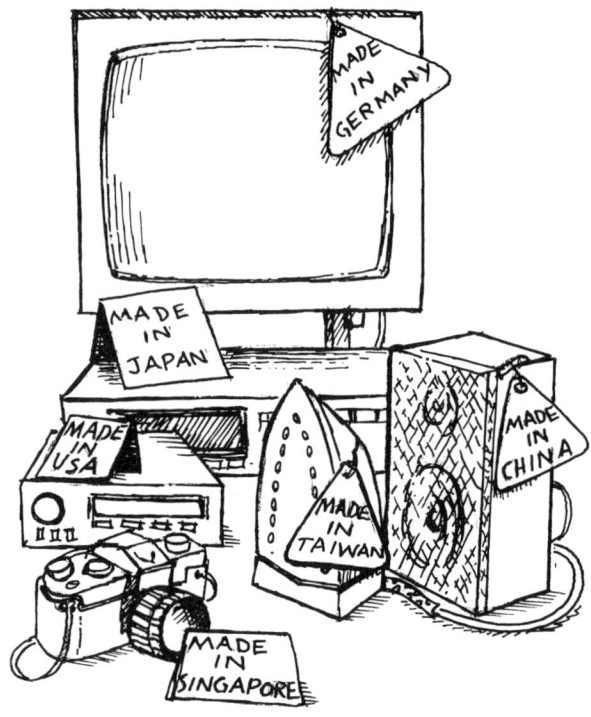

Workshop of the world or a nation of shopkeepers?

Q **When was the last time you saw a British-made motor bike or bought a British-made TV or radio cassette player?**
The signs are all around us that manufacturing industry in Britain is struggling to keep up with cheaper foreign competitors
- the take-over of British motor companies
- the decline of the ship-building and steel industries
- the almost total lack of British-made TVs, videos, fridges and other 'black' and 'white' consumer goods
- the decreasing number of jobs available in skilled engineering, especially in the North of England, the old manufacturing base.

But does any of this matter?

What does the future hold? • Economic change •

New jobs, new attitudes

More and more people are setting up in business to provide services for people:

- Tourism. Record numbers of people visit Britain every year. Hotels, restaurants, leisure facilities and historical places of interest are expanding fast and recruiting workers.

- Will retail stores continue to make good profits, or will spending by visitors and nationals on goods be affected by interest rates or unemployment? How much of what we buy is manufactured here and how much imported? Shops like Marks and Spencer's are expanding overseas.

- Banks, building societies and the financial services of the City of London are recovering from the recession of the 1980s. They have created new jobs and remain the major financial centre in Europe.

But is this enough?

- Children and adults still need education – and to an even higher level if the needs of the changing economy are to be met. People will need technical skills, language skills, keyboard skills and inter-personal skills to make them adaptable in the changing world.

- Educators should always be able to find jobs, and so will people who are good at getting on with and communicating with people.

- Society will still need its carers. Caring for people is labour-intensive. Health and the Social Services will need to recruit workers.

To provide the necessary resources for education and the social and health services Britain will have to earn money, not only through providing services but by designing and manufacturing products which we can sell to the world.

Make sure you are aware of what's going on, learn the right skills and look for the right opportunities.

Job search • group task •

In small groups:

1 Find the Jobs section in the newspaper and list all the headings or categories in the correct column below.

2 Count the total number of jobs under each category and enter them in the correct column.

3 Using the above information answer the four questions in the spaces provided.

4 Be prepared to feed back this information to the rest of the class.

Newspaper	date
Job Category	**number**
Situations General	
Secretarial and Clerical	

1 Which category has the most job vacancies?

2 Which category has the least number of job vacancies?

3 What can you say about the availability of jobs in this area?

4 What else have you noticed about the jobs situation? Have you been surprised in any way?

Job search • pairs tasks •

In pairs:

1 Choose one job from those you have seen which you might want to apply for in the future.

2 Complete the Job Information sheet below.

NB - Not all the information may be provided in the advert, so you might have to leave the space blank or write in N/A (not applicable).

Job information sheet	
Job category	Job title
Permanent/Temporary/Full/Part time (*please delete*)	Salary/Pay
Age range required	Experience needed
Qualifications needed	Job training offered
Perks available (eg extra bonuses, car, creche, etc.)	
Distance travelled: Close to home/Reasonable/Too far (*please delete*)	
Is it part of a YT Scheme?	

Look at the job advert again and discuss with your partner which of the skills below will be needed by someone to do the work: tick the appropriate answer.

	Yes	No	Not sure
Can use machinery	--------	--------	--------
Can work in a team	--------	--------	--------
Can work independently	--------	--------	--------
Can solve problems	--------	--------	--------
Can read	--------	--------	--------
Can write	--------	--------	--------
Can speak clearly	--------	--------	--------
Can give instructions	--------	--------	--------
Can carry out instructions	--------	--------	--------
Can take responsibility	--------	--------	--------
Can make decisions	--------	--------	--------
Can use a keyboard	--------	--------	--------
Can use a computer	--------	--------	--------
Can drive a car	--------	--------	--------
Can confidently meet new people	--------	--------	--------

Job adverts

Use these examples if you don't find any suitable ones in real newspapers.

MANAGERIAL, CLERICAL

BANK CLERK

Management Trainee
Required by local Branch
of leading High Street Bank

Responsibilities include: serving as a counter clerk, meeting the public, keeping records, operating a computer.

Training Opportunities and Prospects for promotion into management

Maths and English GCSE Grade C required

Salary commencing £8,000 pa £150 pw

TRAINEE MANAGER

Required by local D.I.Y. Superstore

Duties: various, checking tills.

Good prospects for hardworking staff.

Wage £7,000 pa (£135 pw) plus overtime

SALES

ELECTRICAL RETAIL STORE

Opportunities for part-time sales staff

If you're confident, enthusiastic and able to get on with all sorts of people we'll give you the training you need. We will make you an expert on our range of leading high-tech electrical goods. You can earn a National Vocational Qualification too.

Hours
11am – 3pm, Mondays to Fridays,
Saturdays optional

Pay
£4.00 p.h. plus commission – guaranteed in the first 8 weeks, incentive competition prizes and generous staff discounts, after a qualifying period

SITUATIONS GENERAL

TELEVISION PRODUCTION CO. REQUIRES

TRAINEE TECHNICAL OPERATORS

to operate a variety of sound and vision equipment

You should have 5 GCSE's at C grade including Maths and Physics

You should be outgoing and enjoy working as a team, remaining calm under pressure.

You should use equipment with skill.

We provide the basic training. If you complete this successfully we will offer you a 6 month contract.

STORES OPERATIVE

Required by Catering Department of Charitable Centre

REQUIRES: person with some stores experience, clean driving licence and own transport. Some overtime may be required.

Free meals whilst on duty.

Good prospects for hardworking staff.

WAGE £156.00 pw 39 hours

CLERICAL

CLERICAL ASSISTANTS

Required by local Housing Association

1. REPAIRS/MAINTENANCE – Duties include dealing with repair ordering, checking invoices & arranging payments. Applicants must possess excellent keyboard and numeracy skills

2. RECEPTION – Work will involve dealing with reception and telephone duties and providing support to the Lettings Section, making maximum use of the word processor.

In addition both posts involve general clerical duties, pleasant telephone manner and a sense of humour

Salary £7698 pa, 19 days holiday, Pension Scheme, Luncheon Vouchers, Flexitime

Made your mind up?

On your own try to decide how you are feeling. Don't panic. You don't have to make up your mind about everything right now.

Which of the following statements would be most true for you right now? Follow the arrows to see what your options are. If you don't understand all of them, check with the *glossary* and the *flow chart*.

I have no idea which career I really want to go in for.

You could:

- get a job to tide you over while you make up your mind.
- do A-levels.
- do a course that gives a taste of several things eg C and G Diploma of Vocational Education (was CPVE) or BTEC.
- talk to lots of people about the jobs they do.
- talk to your Careers Officer.

There are three or four things I'm interested in. I've got some idea of the sort of thing I want to do.

You could:

- choose YT in the field which interests you.
- do A-levels of GCSE re-sits which fit in with your interests.
- do a course like BTEC First, BTEC National or GNVQ which fits in with your interests.
- talk to people who have the sort of jobs you are interested in about what their jobs really involve.
- talk to your Careers Officer.
- look for a job with training which will widen your experience in these sorts of jobs.

I have a pretty clear idea of what I want to do.

You could:

- choose YT in the field which interests you.
- do appropriate A-levels or GCSE re-sits and aim for Higher Education.
- do a course like BTEC First, BTEC National or GNVQ which fits in with your interests.
- find out from your Careers Officer if there are some NVQs that would suit you.
- talk to your Careers Officer.
- look for a job which will lead to the training and promotion you want in your chosen career.
- set up your own business.

Glossary

Use the information below to help you understand the different things you can do after you are sixteen.

Employment   WORK. You may work for yourself or an employer. You may work full-time, part-time, flexi-time or seasonally.

Vocational   JOB-RELATED. This gives you training and qualifications for a particular job or industry.

Academic   EDUCATIONAL. This gives you general qualifications in broad subjects at a basic, advanced or higher level.

A-levels   AN ACADEMIC QUALIFICATION. You can do from one to four subjects. Usually you have to pass GCSE's at a certain grade first. They are offered by School Sixth Forms, Sixth Form Colleges, FE Colleges, and Open Learning or Correspondence courses. A-level success is the usual way of getting a place in Higher Education.

C & G Diploma of Vocational Education   A GENERAL COURSE that usually lasts for one year. It prepares you for working life generally by giving you tasters of what different jobs are like. You also do Work Experience and basic subjects like communication, numeracy and IT. This course is offered by some Sixth Form colleges.

BTEC   VOCATIONAL COURSES offered at Further Education Colleges. They prepare you for specific job areas such as travel and tourism, business or engineering. For BTEC National courses you need four GCSEs at grades A-C or good grades at BTEC First Diploma level.

Polytechnics and Universities accept BTEC National as an entry qualification. Some BTEC courses will also give you GNVQs.

NVQs/GNVQs   VOCATIONAL QUALIFICATIONS which are accepted by industry and commerce. They show what skills you have which are work-related. They cover a wide variety of jobs and you can work towards them while you are in a job, at college or even in your own time. Each NVQ is made up of a number of separate units which set out exactly what the candidate must be able to do and at what standard. You add to them as you go along and try to take them at a higher and higher level. There are no age or entry requirements. GNVQs are more college-based and less related to specific jobs.

YT – Youth Training   VOCATIONAL TRAINING for young people which gives you work experience in a particular job area and the opportunity to gain NVQs. It is open to all young people including those with special needs. There are lots of different types of YT. Some are run by colleges, some by firms or voluntary organisations. Some are 'Employee status', you are officially employed by the company and are paid the rate for the job .

Some are ' apprenticeship training' – you do a three to four year apprenticeship, the first two years of which are YT.

To get on the best YT schemes you must apply early. Ask your Careers Officer for more information.

HND   FULL-TIME NON-DEGREE COURSE at polytechnic or college. Minimum age eighteen.

Degrees   ACADEMIC QUALIFICATIONS offered by Higher Education (universities and polytechnics). You can apply when you are 17 and study for a minimum of three years. There is a huge variety of degree courses. Some are also vocational because they train you for a specific job, eg accountancy or medicine. You can stay on at, or go back to Higher Education to gain post-graduate qualifications such as a teaching qualification, a social work qualification or a higher degree.

Flow chart

In pairs, look at this flow chart. The *glossary* sheet explains what the words mean.

Now check you have understood. Read the *case studies* on page 56 and use coloured pens to draw in career paths for each person. Draw your lines on this sheet.

On another sheet try to draw you own Career Path.

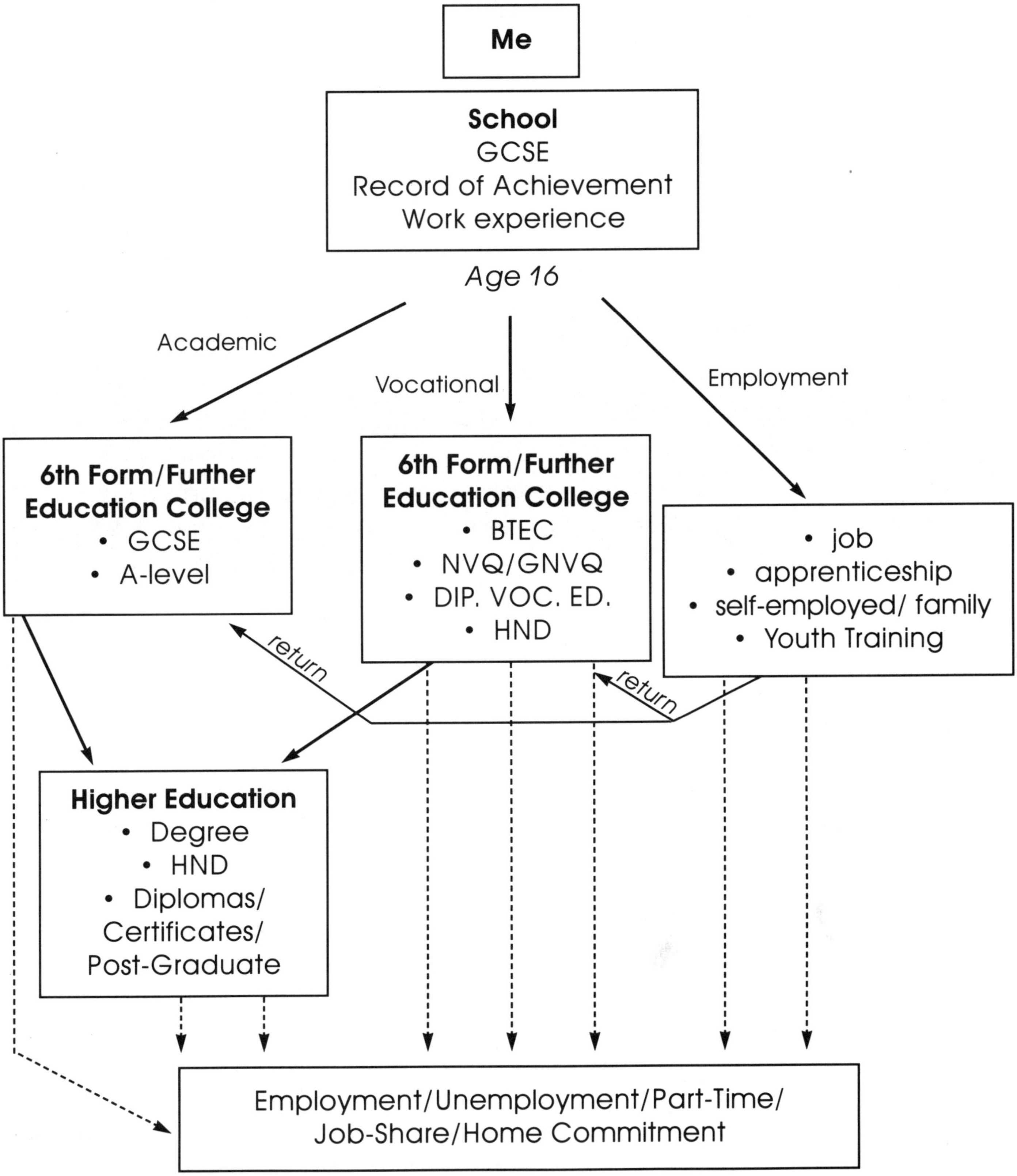

Me

School
GCSE
Record of Achievement
Work experience

Age 16

Academic

Vocational

Employment

6th Form/Further Education College
• GCSE
• A-level

6th Form/Further Education College
• BTEC
• NVQ/GNVQ
• DIP. VOC. ED.
• HND

• job
• apprenticeship
• self-employed/ family
• Youth Training

return

return

Higher Education
• Degree
• HND
• Diplomas/ Certificates/ Post-Graduate

Employment/Unemployment/Part-Time/
Job-Share/Home Commitment

Case studies

Look at these case studies. Try to work out which jobs, training, courses or qualifications these young people need to take if they are to achieve their ambitions.

Using a different colour for each person, draw lines on your flow chart to show what they should do.

Sharon left school with no clear idea of what she wanted to do. At the time she had had enough of school. She got a job in a local shop. After a year she found the work monotonous and no longer challenging. Although the money seemed good at first, she soon realised there were no prospects for promotion. Compared to other jobs, she worked long hours and was poorly paid.

She is now determined to improve her situation by improving her qualifications.

Asif is interested in becoming an engineer. At present he is likely to get between 2 and 4 GCSE passes at Grade C or above. One of these will probably be Maths. Though Physics would be useful, it is doubtful that he will get a Grade C first time.

Claire is 16 and is interested in becoming a dentist. At present she is studying 8 GCSEs and is likely to gain good grades in all of them.

Simon is interested in becoming a chef in a hotel. His attendance at school has been quite poor and he has shown little interest in his academic work. He has done very well in his Food Technology option and is likely to gain a good grade in that subject. He has received good reports from his Work Experience placement in the Catering Department at the local hospital.

18

Job categories checklist

In pairs:

1 For each of the jobs listed below place a tick in the category column in which you think they belong.

2 Decide also whether you think the skills involved in doing this job are easy to transfer to another job or are more specalist.

Job	Description	Medical/ nursing	Technical	Scientific	Secretarial/ clerical	Service/ general	Transfer- able	Spec- ialist
		Category					Skills	
Gardener	I look after the plants inside and outside the hospital.							
Pharmacist	I prepare and dispense medicines and drugs.							
Electronics engineer	I maintain sophisticated electronic equipment such as heart monitors, scanners, etc.							
Doctor	I diagnose the patients' illnesses and decide how to treat them.							
Radiographer	I take and examine X-rays.							
Cook	I prepare meals for the patients and hospital staff.							
Receptionist	I take care of appointments and enquiries from patients and visitors to the hospital.							
Secretary	I type letters and records, etc, for the hospital.							
Librarian	I am in charge of the hospital library and take books to patients							
Social worker	I help people with their problems, eg rent, families and children, while they are in hospital.							
Cleaner	I clean the hospital (wards, corridors, kitchens, waiting rooms, etc.)							
Accountant	I am responsible for the finances of the hospital and for taking care of its budget.							
Midwife	I am a nurse who is trained in childbirth and the care of mothers and babies.							

  **19**

Job	Description	Category						Skills	
		Medical/ nursing	Technical	Scientific	Secretarial/ clerical	Service/ general	Transfer-able	Spec-ialist
Physiotherapist	I treat patients with exercise and heat.							
Machine fitter	I maintain and install machinery.							
Disc jockey	I run the hospital radio service and play requests for patients.							
Carpenter	I make and repair wooden furniture, doors, windows and gates at the hospital.							
Records clerk	I look after the records about the patients							
Storekeeper	I am responsible for keeping and ordering supplies for the hospital.							
Security guard	I patrol the hospital building and check the doors etc for security.							
Surgeon	I am a doctor who specialises in surgical treatment: carrying out operations.							
Computer operator	I enter and store all kinds of information for the hospital onto the computer and access it when it is needed.							
Porter	I move things around in the hospital – patients, beds, and food, etc.							
Administrator	I run the hospital and represent it at a higher level,							
Anaesthetist	I give anaesthetics to patients during operations and make sure they are breathing properly.							
Nurse	I am trained to look after people on the wards and give patients the treatment decided by the doctors.							
Medical photographer	I take photographs for doctors and students.							
Laundry worker	I take care of the dirty washing.							
Ambulance driver	I take patients to and from hospital and give emergency medical treatment.							
Nursing officer	I am in charge of the nursing staff.							

58

Work and pay • what do you know? •

Answer question one individually and questions two and three in pairs.

1 Read the list of terms below and tick the box if you've heard the term.
2 Discuss with a partner what you think each term means, then write down the answer.
3 Check if you were correct by looking at the next page.

1 Tax Code	☐	....
2 National Insurance	☐	....
3 Income Tax	☐	....
4 Superannuation/ Pension Contribution	☐	....
5 Union Fees	☐	....
6 Gross/Net Pay	☐	....
7 Tax Year	☐	....

Work and pay • information •

Use the information below to check your answers to the questions on the previous page.

1   Tax Code

Every worker is given a tax code when he or she is first paid. This code tells you how much you are allowed to earn before you pay tax, eg:

Personal Allowance	£4,195	=	419 L
Married Couple's Allowance	£1,900	=	190 H

- Notice the last figure of the earnings is missed off to determine the tax code
- The letter after your number defines your status, eg:

  L   =   single personal allowance

  H   =   married couple's allowance – allowed to one of the couple on top of the personal allowance

  X   =   emergency code, ie you haven't been assessed yet.

2   National Insurance

This is a deduction from your salary by the government used to pay for the health service, sick pay, social services, unemployment benefits, etc.

3   Income Tax

This is a deduction from your salary by the government. It is paid as a percentage of your earnings after deductions have been made. The percentage can change from year to year. It is used by the government to run the country, eg to pay for defence, roads, civil service, etc.

4   Superannuation/Pension contribution

This is the money taken from your wages to help pay for a pension when you retire.

5   Union Fees

It is advisable to be a member of a union to help protect your rights as a worker. Some unions allow you to pay the subscription every week or month through your employer.

6   Gross/Net pay

Gross pay is your total weekly/monthly wages before any deductions have been made. Net pay is how much you are left with (take-home pay) after all the deductions have been made.

7   Tax Year

The tax year runs from the 6th of April to the 5th of April the following year. Income tax forms may be sent at the start of the tax year.
Tax Month 1 = April;   Tax Month 12 = March.

Work and pay • payslip •

Complete this worksheet either individually or in pairs.

1 Look at the copy of a Payslip below.

2 Answer the questions about it.

Hourly Rate in Pence	TAX CODE	TAX MONTH	TAX YEAR	NAME		DEPT	MAN NO
340	278L	9	94/95	Smith A		36193	75231

CUMULATIVE AMOUNTS IN CURRENT TAX YEAR					THIS WEEK/MONTH		BANK	
Gross Taxable pay	Tax paid	Nat insce	Supn	Supnble pay	Gross taxable pay	Subnble pay	Account	Code
4651.29	570.00	291.04	270.04	4651.29	677.05	677.05	5582412	7613

Item code	£	Item code	£	Item code	£	Net pay £
1	496.87	3	180.18	31	4.00*	493.39
21	101.00*	22	38.04*	32	40.62*	

C. Tr Form L317   *Indicates a deduction from Pay   See overleaf for explanation of codes

Item Code PAYMENTS	Item Code PAYMENTS (cont.)	Item Code DEDUCTIONS	Item Code DEDUCTIONS (cont.)
1 Basic Pay	11 Boots/clothing	21 Income Tax	31 Trade Union Subscription
2 Miscellaneous/Holiday Pay	12 Car Allowance	22 National Insurance	32 Contribution to Pension
3 Overtime Pay	13 Meals/Travel Allowance	23 NI Sick Benefit	Fund
4 Supplementary Allowances	14 Statutory Sick Pay	24 Court O	33 Social Fund
5 Bonus	15 Other Allowances	25	

1 What is the Basic Pay of A. Smith? £

2 What is the take-home (net) pay of A. Smith? £

3 What were the 4 deductions taken from the salary this month?
a   c
b   d

4 How much was deducted this month? £

5 What is A. Smith's Tax Code? ....

6 How is the money paid to A. Smith at the end of the month?
Underline the one correct answer. *Bank/Cash/Bank Giro/Cheque*

7 What month is this Pay Slip for?
Underline the correct answer. *April/September/December/March*

8 What should A. Smith do with the Pay Slip once it has been received?
Underline the correct answers.
a *throw it away*   c *return it to the employer*
b *keep it for reference*   d *check it*

Quiz sheet

Can you answer these questions?

1 A future prospective employer wants you to send a CV. What is this?

2 Write down the addresses and phone numbers of two Area Careers Offices near you.

3 What is a P45?

4 What is the difference between FE and HE?

5 What is a bridging allowance? Who is entitled to it? How do you claim it?

6 Write down the address of the local Citizens Advice Bureau.

7 How do you claim Housing Benefit?

8 How can you claim Unemployment Benefit? Explain.

9 Can you claim Income Support?

10 What is a Contract of Employment? What is in it?

11 In a formal letter if you start Dear Sir or Madam, how do you end it?

12 You are applying for a job. Who do you give as your referees?

13 You want a holiday job. What is the best way to go about it?

14 For how many years after leaving school do your parents still get Child Benefit if you are still in full-time education?

15 What is Statutory Sick Pay?

16 What does GNVQ stand for?

17 Find the address of the Equal Opportunities Commission.

18 Find the address of your nearest Job Centre.

19 One of your friends is leaving home because of difficulties. Suggest an address which would provide help.

Personal & Social Education
and cross-curricular themes

Self-study pack

Term 1 Module 2

Careers

name

form   date

Application forms

Application forms come in many different sizes, requiring more or less information. There are some examples here for you to practise on.

1 Complete the example on page 2, following the instructions

2 Complete the application form for employment on pages 3 and 4 and the application for a course on pages 5 and 6.

3 After completing these two you may like to fill in a real application for a course or a job which you want to pursue.

4 Some application forms give you a space to write about yourself and your interests. Summarise the information from your personal statement in your *Record of Achievement* and use it to fill the box below.

Remember to make yourself sound interesting and suitable for the course or job you are applying for.

Remarks

Please give details of your interests and hobbies and any other information you feel will help your application.

Application forms • continued •

1 Follow instructions.
2 Make a photocopy to practise first, or use a pencil.
3 Use black ink or type.
4 Write neatly.
5 Check the closing date, apply in time.
6 Make copies before you send it off.

Almost all application forms require the following basic information.

Job title	**Permanent/Temporary/Full/Part time** *(please delete)*
Surname	**First names**
Age and date of birth	**National Insurance Number**
Address	
Post code	**Home telephone number**

Are you disabled?   YES ☐   NO ☐

Do you require any special arrangements eg adaptations to premises or equipment *(please list requirements)*

Secondary education
Qualifications *(give details of exams taken, or to be taken, and results if known)*
Work experience or employment

Application for employment

Use your own handwriting Strictly confidential

Employment now sought

Surname (BLOCK LETTERS)

Christian name(s) in full

Full Postal Address (BLOCK LETTERS)

Date of birth *Note: You will be required to produce a birth certificate*

Married or single	Nationality

Full time education

Date		Name and type of school	Standard reached, examinations passed
from	to		

Training *Give details of courses taken since full-time education ceased*

Date		College	Subject and Qualification	Type of Course
from	to			

Application for employment •continued •

Full particulars of your Employment over the last 3 years 67

Names and addresses of Employers	Dates		Duties	Reason for leaving
	from	to		

Health
Office use only

Height, without shoes . . . . . feet . . . . . inches Weight . . . . . stones . . . . . lbs	
Is your eyesight good? With glasses . . . . . .Without glasses	
Is your hearing good?	
Have you suffered from -	
fits	
rupture	
any serious illness	
any accident	
If registered under The Disabled Persons Act 1944 give Registered No	

Leisure interests *(hobbies, sports, clubs, etc.)*

The information I have given above is true to the best of my knowledge and belief.

Signed .... Date ....

For official use

Suitability
(Tick as appropriate)

     highly suitable   probably suitable

     suitable   unsuitable

Comments covering experience, special qualities, etc.

Application for a course

Application form for post-16 education at a school or college

Please complete this form in BLACK ink and in CAPITAL LETTERS

1 Surname .... Other Names ....

2 Name of parent/guardian ....

3 Address...

....

....

postcode .... Telephone number ....

4 Date of birth .... Male/female ....

5 Ethnic origin *(Please note this information will only be used for statistical purposes.)*

Please tick the most appropriate box:

☐ White	☐ Indian
☐ Black Caribbean	☐ Pakistani
☐ Black African	☐ Bangladeshi
☐ Black Other	☐ Chinese

Other *(please specify)* ....

6 Name of present school ....

7 Name of school/college you wish to apply to ....

8 Course you wish to apply for. *(Please refer to the 'After 16' booklet and discuss your choice with your Careers Teacher or Careers Officer – if you are not sure which course is best for you at this stage, please put 'NOT SURE')* ....

....

....

....

....

9 Interests and positions of responsibility, for example, sports, music, part-time jobs.

....

....

....

....

....

....

....

Application for a course • continued •

10 Career interests *(Please tell us if you have any career ideas at this stage.)*

....

....

11 Health/disability *(Please give brief details of any aspects of your health or any disability which you feel ought to be brought to our notice.)*

....

....

12

Part a	*Part b*	
To be completed by the applicant:	To be completed by the school:	
Subjects being studied	Course and level GCSE/unit credits/others	Estimated results

13 Reference by headteacher *(Please comment on the suitability of the candidate for the courses requested and/or submit a summative document where appropriate.)*

- *Attendance*   Below average   average   above average
- *Punctuality*   Below average   average   above average
- *Comments on the course choices and any additional information:*

14 Headteacher's signature ....   Date ....

15 Student's signature ....   Date ....

Please take your Record of Achievement, if you have one, when you are invited for interview to discuss your choice.

Writing a letter of application

Sometimes you may need to write a letter of application. You do this when:

- you need to provide more information about yourself than there is space for on your application form
- you want to stand out to a college or employer
- you think your letter may be opened by the person who will be responsible for choosing who gets the job.

When you need to write your own covering letter or letter of application, get some writing paper from your form tutor.

Use the layout and punctuation shown here.

---

reference number, if given in the advert

CA/43/

your address, telephone number and date

13 Harbour Rd
Longsight
Manchester M13 9EQ
13th February 19_ _

name and address of person you are writing to

Mr N.S.Bell,
Bell and Co
Brooklands Way
London N3 4JT

miss a line

Dear Mr Bell,
I should like to apply for the position of trainee clerical assistant as advertised in the Evening News last Friday.

you write something about why you would be suitable for this particular job

clear paragraphs

This job is of particular interest to me because I am keen to find commercial employment where I will be given the opportunity to train further and gain professional qualifications. Although I have as yet no experience in this type of work, my part-time employment as a Supermarket Cashier has provided a valuable opportunity to meet members of the public and deal with accounts and finance.

clear paragraphs

I enclose my CV I shall be pleased to provide any further details required. I am free to come for interview at any time.

Yours sincerely

A.R. Anwar **your signature**
A.R. Anwar **your name, printed**

Writing a covering letter

You may need to write a covering letter. You do this when:

- you want to ask for more information about a job or a course you have seen in an advert (and perhaps ask for an application form)
- you want a prospectus from a college
- you are returning a completed application form.

Remember

1 Use good quality paper.

2 If you know the name of the person you are writing to, eg Mrs Edwards, sign your letter *Yours sincerely* followed by your name. If you write 'Dear Sir or Madam', then end the letter *Yours faithfully*.

3 Write the letter out in rough first. Then check the spelling and punctuation. Keep your letter brief.

Dear Sir/Madam

With reference to the advertisement in the Evening News last Monday, for the post of Care Assistant, please send further details and an application form. I enclose a stamped addressed envelope.

Yours faithfully

D.E. Porter

Dear Mrs Edwards

I enclose a completed application form for the post of Care Assistant Grade 2. I look forward to hearing from you.

D.E. Porter

Dear Sir/Madam

Please send your current College Prospectus and any further information you have on the BTEC National course in Engineering.

Yours faithfully,

D.E. Porter

Telephone skills

The next three pages aim to improve your ability to get the careers information you need over the telephone.

Read this example

Shahana has heard of a course that her local FE College offers. She thinks she may be interested but doesn't know enough about it to make up her mind. Also she doesn't know if she has the right qualifications to be able to start the course. She would like to visit the college to talk to the course tutor.

She arranges with her careers teacher to use the telephone. . .

Shahana	Hello. My name's Shahana Ashraf and I'm interested in. . .
Switchboard Operator	Which department?
Shahana	Oh, er, I think it's called Business and Finance.
Switchboard Operator	Putting you through now.
Voice	Hello, Business Studies.
Shahana	Hello. My name's Shahana Ashraf and I'm interested in your BTEC course in Business and Finance.
Voice	Are you a student?
Shahana	Yes, I'm 16 and still at school.
Voice	Well, you need our Student Welfare Section. I'll put you back to the switchboard.
Shahana	No, just a minute. I need some information from someone in your department. I'd like to speak to the person who's course tutor for BTEC Business or Finance.
Voice	BTEC First or BTEC National?
Shahana	BTEC First I think. I'm not sure if I've got the right qualifications for the National.
Voice	Right, well, you need to speak to Ms Roberts. She'll sort you out. I'll see if she's available. . . No, I'm sorry. She's teaching until 2.30pm. Could you ring back later?
Shahana	Yes, all right. Does she have her own extension number?
Voice	Yes. You could try her on 230. If that doesn't work, try 231 which is the general office number for our section.
Shahana	Thank you very much for your help.

How did she do? Remember you too may have to speak to several people before you get the person you want. Underline the information that she needed to make a note of as she was making the call. If you are confident you could do as well, go on to page 11 and try it out. If you are still unsure, imagine you are Shahana ringing back later for the information she wants. Write a new script on page 10.

Telephone skills • continued •

This sheet will help you gain confidence when speaking over the telephone to people you don't know.

You have already read about Shahana who has to ring back to ask to speak to the course tutor.

Jot down here the main things Shahana wants to know

Who should she ask for?

Extension
Number?

Switchboard Operator

Shahana

Switchboard Operator   Putting you through now

Voice

Shahana

Voice

Shahana

Voice

Shahana

Voice

Shahana

Voice

Shahana

Now try your own example. Turn to page 11.

Telephone skills

This sheet will prepare you to get some information by speaking over the telephone to people you don't know.

Decide whether you are going to **a)** ring about a post-16 course, **b)** ring about work experience. Underline your choice, then read the correct box.

---

*Fill in these details if you have chosen the **post-16 course***

You want to speak to the course tutor for . . . .

You wish to arrange a visit to find out if it is the right course for you. Jot down notes of what you want to say. Be prepared to give details about yourself.

---

*Fill in these details if you have chosen the **work experience***

Your school has arranged a work experience for you at

. . . .

You want to speak to someone there who can give you more details.
Where is it exactly? To whom should you report when you get there?
What are the starting and finishing times? Should you bring a packed lunch?
What clothes are suitable? Jot down notes of what you want to say. Be prepared to give details about yourself.

When ready, ask your teacher if you can try out your request on a real telephone. Tape yourself.

And now for the rest of your life

Objectives

To provide students with the opportunity:

1 to reflect on aspects of their personal and social development programme which have been important to them

2 to choose which concerns they still wish to follow up in the remaining months of year 11

3 to organise themselves into effective learning groups.

Methodology

Lesson 1 Students review their programme and indicate those modules which were of greatest importance. Students then consider their current needs. After group discussion of current needs, the groups and subsequently the class decide to follow this programme or set their own programme.

Resources Student Booklet (1 per student)   77

And now for the rest of your life

Lesson 1
A time to reflect

1 Recall the content and methods of the programme so far while students turn to *student booklet* page 1 *Looking back*.

Example 'You have been following a Pastoral Programme for five years now. During that time you've looked at a number of issues and developed skills which will have helped your personal and social development. Which have been most important to you personally?'

Students colour or indicate their choices.

2 Ask students to think about their needs now. They have a term left of work with this class.

Are there:

- any areas they wish they had done more on?
- any important areas they have completely missed so far?
- any areas they wish to go back to now that they are older?

There are perhaps also some ways of learning that suit them particularly. On *student booklet* page 2 *And now for the rest of your life* are some of the areas which they may consider need more attention. In groups of three, students discuss and record preferences about areas of study and methods.

3 Now it is time for students to share in choosing what to do. Firstly there should be a class discussion to bring together the reactions and concerns of the groups. Secondly the students must decide what topic or topics they would like to investigate and study and how they want to go about it. They can study either or both of the modules herewith, as the whole of their course of study or as part of a course of study. They may decide on other areas of concern and set about tasks to investigate and study the topic or topics. They must also decide if this investigation and study is to be undertaken individually, in small or large groups, what tasks are to be undertaken, how the tasks are to be reported on and the timescale.

It is suggested that at least one full lesson is given to this discussion. At the end of the discussion or during the next lesson the programme should be displayed in the classroom. It should include information about tasks to be undertaken, targets for learning and deadlines. Any information regarding groups should also be included.

Personal & Social Education
and cross-curricular themes

Student Booklet

Term 2 Module 3

A time to reflect

name

form   date

Looking back

Over the past five years you have learned about many issues and developed new skills. Colour in the ones that *you* have found most interesting and important.

Group Discussion

First Aid

Relationships

Citizenship

Healthy Living

Careers

Living by the Rules

Sex-stereotyping

Study Skills

Sex Education

Conflict

Parenthood

Role Play

You and the Law

Addressing the Class

Feeling Positive

Leisure

Designing Posters and Cartoons

Review Day

Expressing your Feelings

Stress

Social Skills

Case Studies (what would it be like if. . .)

A.I.D.S

Watching videos

Self-Assessment

Equal Opportunities

Interviews

Record of Achievement

Health

Self-Presentation

?	?	?

And now for the rest of your life!

In groups of three discuss what you think you need to cover this term. Indicate your choices in order of preference – 1,2,3, etc.

Here are some areas which may still need more attention. What do you think?

Drug education - weighing the risks

Going to the doctor

Complementary medicines

The environment

Sexuality

Parenthood

Politics

First Aid

Stress and preparing for exams

Finding and setting up a home

?

?

It's time for you to share in choosing what we do in these lessons and also how we do it. It will be more up to you to organise it, according to how you learn best.

Do you learn best . . .

watching videos?   by brainstorming?

discussing?

through role play?

individual?   working as a team?

through research

with others?   working on your own?

Health and welfare

Objectives

To provide students with the opportunity:

1 to focus on future decisions, having considered their own values, i.e. to be sexually active or not, to use contraception or not

2 to inform students about contraception and sexually transmitted disease

3 to establish how people get sexually transmitted diseases and how to reduce the risk

4 to discuss responsibility and moral values in relationships

5 to apply the knowledge they have gained to decision-making in personal relationships.

Methodology

Lesson 1 Discussion of the attitude of different faiths to contraception followed by students exercising their opinions and explaining why to a partner. Practical explanation and where possible demonstration of various contraceptive devices. Completion of reference sheet. Students complete *self-evaluation* page. (This lesson will probably take more than one lesson.)

Lesson 2 Students answer a questionnaire and check their answers in pairs. After a discussion in pairs students examine real-life situations, and report back to the class. Class participation in values continues. Students complete *self-evaluation* page.

Lesson 3 Brainstorm attitudes. In groups answer questions relating to case studies, then bring answers to class discussion. Class review. Students complete *Attitude quiz*. Students complete *self-evaluation* page.

Resources

Student Booklet (1 per student)   87

Resource box, containing pictures and packets of
various contraceptive devices.
School nurse often very helpful.
Health Promotion Units sometimes lend out the Brook Advisory
Service Pack which contains many contraceptive devices.
NB It is useful to have some other adult support for these lessons so that the
teacher can get round to all the pupils. Think about co-teaching with your Head
of Year/school nurse or someone else who could back you up in this lesson.

Health and Welfare

Lesson 1
Contraception: the facts

1 Distribute *student booklet.*

Point out that adult life involves making various decisions concerning our one-to-one relationships which can have an effect on our health and welfare. To help us make those decisions we each need to be clear about our own values and beliefs. This lesson is designed to let us consider our individual values regarding contraception, and to inform ourselves about different contraceptive methods.

2 Ask all students to look at *student booklet* page 1. Read and explain the information about the beliefs of the different faiths. If you know there are other faiths than these represented in your class, try to find some relevant information.

There is no such thing as a consensus of values on these matters – what does matter is that we have each carefully considered our opinions.

In the light of this ask students to complete the sheet with their opinions and then to turn to a partner and explain why they think what they do.

3 Arrange chairs in semi-circle. Teacher sits in middle with Resource box. Show devices or pictures and ask if students know correct names for them. Then, using *Teachers' notes* page 84 for reference, give more detail about how each method works and any drawbacks or health hazards. Answer students' questions.

4 Students return to desks and turn to *student booklet* pages 2 and 3. The task is to create a correct reference sheet by sorting out the correct information and writing it onto their blank sheet.

Student booklet page 4 is for further information.

Teacher moves round making sure that the sheets are correct and answering student questions.

5 Ask students to complete the *self-evaluation* page.

Lesson 2
Sexually transmitted diseases: the facts

1 Explain objectives of lesson and ask each student to check what he or she already knows by completing *student booklet* pages 5 and 6.

In pairs students check the answers by referring to *student booklet* pages 7 and 8. Poor readers should not be placed together. Teacher may need to go through the information, especially with poorer readers, to make sure they understand.

2 Class discussion – how can the risk of catching STDs be reduced?

3 In twos, examine the situations and answer the questions on *student booklet* page 9.

4 Feedback: Is there a consensus on what action is most appropriate for each situation?

5 *Either*

Read out statements on STDs. Students place themselves at either the **agree** or the **disagree** ends of the room. They can discuss their views with someone near them and someone from the other side.

or

Students form groups of five or six and complete *student booklet* page 10.

6 Class discussion.

7 Ask students to complete the *self-evaluation* sheet.

Lesson 3
Health and welfare dilemmas

1 Brief class on objectives of the lesson, i.e. that they have received a lot of information about contraception and STDs but this lesson will require them to apply that information to decisions made by individuals and couples about their behaviour.

2 Brainstorm the possible consequences of making a relationship sexual.

Teacher refers to page 85 *What are the consequences* to ensure all suggestions are adequately covered.

3 Form groups of five. Each group answers the questions from at least three *Health and welfare case studies* from *student booklet* pages 11 to 14. They will need to apply all they know about relationships, contraception and STDs in order to do this.

4 Feedback from each group. Collate answers, correct misinformation and ask for further responses if necessary.

5 Class review: Which groups had really catered for protecting people's health and welfare in their answers to the case studies?

6 Individuals test their own attitudes by completing *student booklet* page 15 *Attitude quiz*.

7 Ask students to complete the *self-evaluation* page.

NOTES

- From our experience, Muslim students who are observing Ramadan will not wish to study this module. The Co-ordinator needs to check the dates of Ramadan each year to ensure that these particular lessons do not fall during Ramadan.

- It may be useful to refer to this unit with year 10 students when they are working on module 4, *Relationships* or module 5, *Parenthood*.

Contraception – the facts

These are the right answers! Use them to check if students have the facts right.

Name	What it is	How it works	Comments
condom	rubber sheath put over erect penis	prevents sperm from entering vagina and reaching the egg	This is the only contraceptive which protects against STD including HIV infection. It is more reliable as a contraceptive and for protection against disease when used with spermicide. Not 100% reliable. Can interrupt love-making. No side effects.
'morning after' pill	hormone pills taken within 72 hours of unprotected sex	prevents the fertilised egg from implanting in the uterus and growing into a baby	It can be used in an emergency to prevent a pregnancy. Not suitable for regular use.
diaphragm or cap	rubber cap that is covered with spermicide and placed over the cervix before sex. Left in place for 6 hours after sex.	prevents the sperm from entering the uterus and reaching the egg	It must be used with a spermicide. Needs careful fitting. No side effects.
withdrawal	man pulls penis out of vagina before he ejaculates	sperm do not meet egg because man ejaculates outside vagina	There is a high risk of pregnancy. (Some semen can enter vagina before ejaculation.)
vasectomy	simple surgery to cut vas deferens	sperm can no longer be ejaculated, only spermless semen	This is a permanent way of making sure a man fathers no more children.
female sterilisation	surgery to cut fallopian tubes	eggs can no longer reach sperm	This is a permanent way of making sure a woman has no more children. Possible heavy periods. Sometimes fertility returns.
I.U.D. or coil	plastic/metal device inserted into uterus	prevents fertilised egg from implanting in the uterus and growing into a baby	This is only suitable for women who have had a baby. Risk of pelvic infection and heavy periods. Occasional failures.
injectable methods	injection of a hormone every 3 months	changes woman's body so that fertilised egg can't implant in the uterus	This is unpredictable as you can't predict when fertility will return. Possibly unpleasant side-effects such as irregular bleeding.
oral contraceptive or combined pill	pill containing 2 female hormones taken daily as instructed	prevents ovulation (release of egg)	Is the most effective preventer of pregnancy if taken as directed. Needs monitoring for side effects. Not for women over 45 or for women over 35 who smoke. Not safe to be taken by all women.
'natural' methods/ rhythm method	close observation of woman's body and no sex when fertile	relies on natural cycle of woman's body to allow couple to avoid sex when she is fertile	Is the only method allowed by R.C. Church. Only works if woman has regular periods. No artificial barriers or hormones.

What are the consequences?

pregnancy: wanted-
    unwanted

pleasure: giving and receiving

cervical cancer

STDs-HIV

Herpes/warts

orgasms

Gonorrhoea

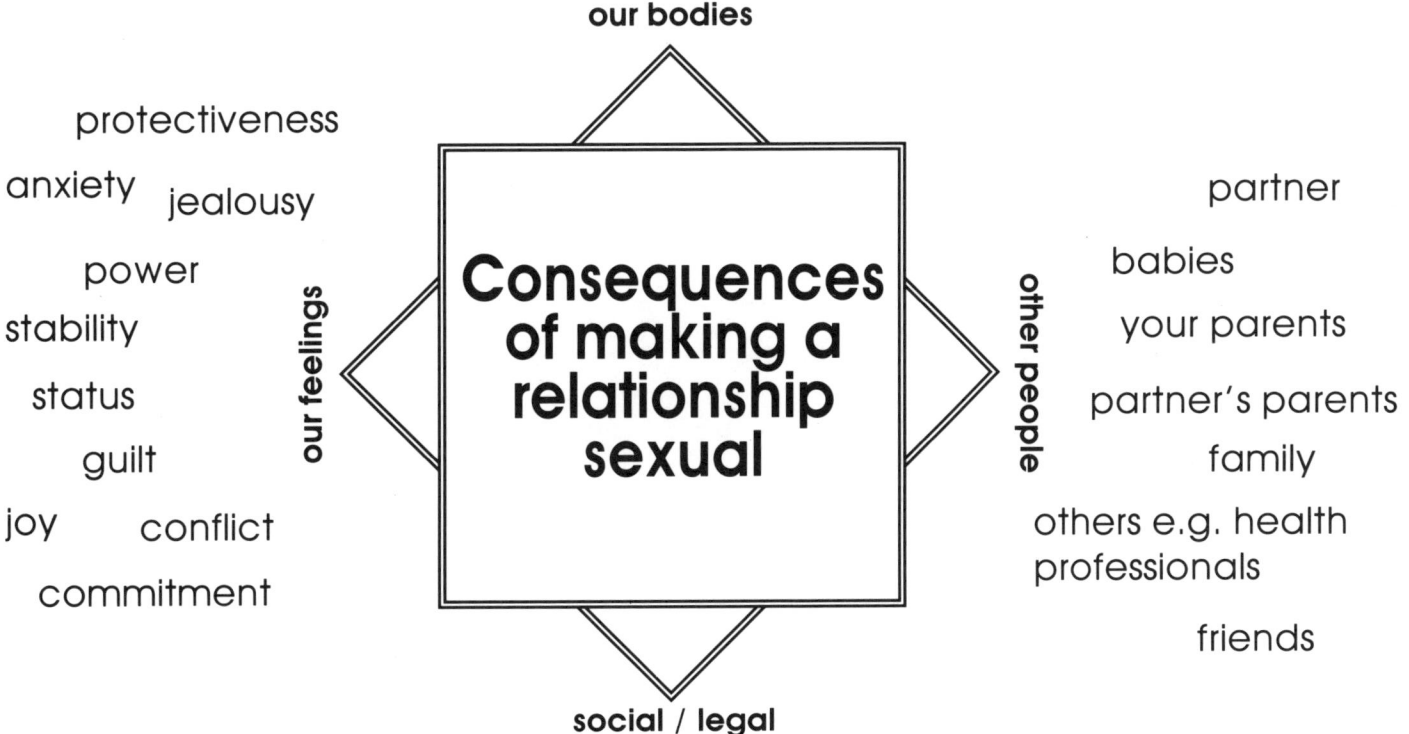

our bodies

protectiveness

anxiety jealousy

power

stability

status

guilt

joy   conflict

commitment

our feelings

Consequences of making a relationship sexual

other people

partner

babies

your parents

partner's parents

family

others e.g. health professionals

friends

social / legal

age of consent
- heterosexual
- homosexual

reputations

family structures

religious values

moral values

cultural values

National Health Service

Personal & Social Education
and cross-curricular themes

Student Booklet

Term 2 Module 4

Health and welfare

name

form   date

In your opinion

Different faiths have different views on whether or when it is acceptable to use contraception. Below are some simplified explanations. For more advice, check with your family, religious teacher, or someone who has knowledge of what these views are.

Note: All faiths see sex outside marriage as wrong, therefore it is wrong to use contraception to allow or promote promiscuous behaviour.

Christian Churches

Roman Catholic Church

Sex within marriage is a blessing but its purpose is to create children. This must always be possible. No artificial means of preventing this is acceptable. The only acceptable method is the rhythm method, 'natural family planning'.

Other Christian Churches

These hold various views but generally accept the use of contraception within marriage. Those who feel strongly that abortion is wrong may think that use of the I.U.D, coil or 'morning after pill' is unacceptable because they prevent a fertilised egg from implanting and could be seen as a very early abortion.

Islam

Sex within marriage is a blessing and having children is a prime purpose of marriage. In general therefore it is wrong for individuals to try to go against this by using contraception. However, married couples must respect and cater for each other's health and welfare. It is important that both partners are happy. There may be times when, in order to safeguard the wife's health, couples might consider using contraception to, for instance, space pregnancies.

It must be remembered that permanent change to the body - for instance sterilisation - is wrong. The I.U.D./ coil and injectable methods may present problems because they can cause unpredictable bleeding in the middle of a woman's menstrual cycle.

Judaism (Orthodox)

Sex within marriage is a blessing and procreation is a command for men. Men should use no form of contraception. Couples may consider it necessary, in certain cases, to use female methods of contraception in order to maintain a woman's physical or mental health. In these cases they should seek advice from a rabbi.

The I.U.D./coil and injectable methods may present problems because they can cause unpredictable bleeding in the middle of a woman's menstrual cycle.

In your opinion

Here are some different reasons people give for using contraception. Do you think any of them are acceptable?

	Acceptable	Unacceptable	not sure
• to space pregnancies so that the mother's health does not suffer			
• because couple are not ready for a baby			
• because couple don't want any children			
• to prevent birth of a baby which may be handicapped by a genetic condition			
• to protect themselves against sexually transmitted diseases			
• because it would be dangerous for the mother to have a baby			

Jumbled contraception reference

The comments boxes are jumbled up. Put them in the right place on the next page.

Name	What it is	How it works	Comments
condom	rubber sheath put over erect penis	prevents sperm from entering vagina and reaching the egg	This is a permanent way of making sure a woman has no more children. Possible heavy periods. Sometimes fertility returns.
'morning after' pill	hormone pills taken within 72 hours of unprotected sex	prevents the fertilised egg from implanting in the uterus and growing into a baby	It can be used in an emergency to prevent a pregnancy. Not suitable for regular use.
diaphragm or cap	rubber cap that is covered with spermicide and placed over the cervix before sex. Left in place for 6 hours after sex.	prevents the sperm from entering the uterus and reaching the egg	This is the only contraceptive which protects against STD including HIV infection. It is more reliable as a contraceptive and for protection against disease when used with spermicide. Not 100% reliable. Can interrupt love-making. No side effects.
withdrawal	man pulls penis out of vagina before he ejaculates	sperm do not meet egg because man ejaculates outside vagina	It must be used with a spermicide. Needs careful fitting. No side effects.
vasectomy	simple surgery to cut vas deferens	sperm can no longer be ejaculated, only spermless semen	There is a high risk of pregnancy. (Some semen can enter vagina before ejaculation.)
female sterilisation	surgery to cut fallopian tubes	eggs can no longer reach sperm	This is unpredictable as you can't predict when fertility will return. Possibly unpleasant side-effects such as irregular bleeding.
I.U.D. or coil	plastic/metal device inserted into uterus	prevents fertilised egg from implanting in the uterus and growing into a baby	Is the only method allowed by R.C. Church. Only works if woman has regular periods. No artificial barriers or hormones
injectable methods	injection of a hormone every 3 months	changes woman's body so that fertilised egg can't implant in the uterus	This is a permanent way of making sure a man fathers no more children.
oral contraceptive or combined pill	pill containing 2 female hormones taken daily as instructed	prevents ovulation (release of egg)	This is only suitable for women who have had a baby. Risk of pelvic infection and heavy periods. Occasional failures.
'natural' methods/ rhythm method	close observation of woman's body and no sex when fertile	relies on natural cycle of woman's body to allow couple to avoid sex when she is fertile	Is the most effective preventer of pregnancy if taken as directed. Needs monitoring for side effects. Not for women over 45 or for women over 35 who smoke. Not safe to be taken by all women.

Contraception reference

Find the information to go in the comment boxes, and complete the sheet.

Name	What it is	How it works	Comments
condom	rubber sheath put over erect penis	prevents sperm from entering vagina and reaching the egg	
'morning after' pill	hormone pills taken within 72 hours of unprotected sex	prevents the fertilised egg from implanting in the uterus and growing into a baby	
diaphragm or cap	rubber cap that is covered with spermicide and placed over the cervix before sex. Left in place for 6 hours after sex.	prevents the sperm from entering the uterus and reaching the egg	
withdrawal	man pulls penis out of vagina before he ejaculates	sperm do not meet egg because man ejaculates outside vagina	
vasectomy	simple surgery to cut vas deferens	sperm can no longer be ejaculated, only spermless semen	
female sterilisation	surgery to cut fallopian tubes	eggs can no longer reach sperm	
I.U.D. or coil	plastic/metal device inserted into uterus	prevents fertilised egg from implanting in the uterus and growing into a baby	
injectable methods	injection of a hormone every 3 months	changes woman's body so that fertilised egg can't implant in the uterus	
oral contraceptive or combined pill	pill containing 2 female hormones taken daily as instructed	prevents ovulation (release of egg)	
'natural' methods/ rhythm method	close observation of woman's body and no sex when fertile	relies on natural cycle of woman's body to allow couple to avoid sex when she is fertile	

90

Where they can be obtained

These boxes contain more information. Find the right information that goes with each method and add it to your blank sheet. You will then have a complete reference sheet.

Name	Where they can be obtained
condom	Widely available from supermarkets, chemists, slot machines, etc. Cost - about 25p each, or FREE from family planning clinics. To be effective must be used carefully and disposed of safely. Should be date-stamped and kite-marked. Those which contain spermicide are more reliable.
'morning after' pill	Free from family planning clinics. Must be taken within 72 hours of unprotected sex.
diaphragm or cap	Free from family planning clinics. Spermicide also free or can be bought from chemists. Common brands of spermicide include Orthogynol and Orthocreme.
withdrawal	Free.
vasectomy	Operation on N.H.S or privately. Counselling available at family planning clinics.
female sterilisation	Operation on N.H.S. Counselling available at family planning clinics.
I.U.D. or coil	Free from family planning clinics. Must be fitted by a skilled doctor. Not usually suitable for young women. May not be suitable for some religious groups because it can cause irregular bleeding
injectable methods	Free from family planning clinics. Not usually suitable for young women. May not be suitable fopr some religious groups because it can cause irregular bleeding.
oral contraceptive or combined pill	Free from family planning clinics or GPs Attendance at family planning clinics usually preferable in order to get full range of check-ups, eg blood pressure and cervical smear tests.
'natural' methods/ rhythm method	Free advice on how it works from family planning clinics and Catholic Marriage Advisory Service.

Questionnaire

Follow the instructions to find out how much you know about STDs.

1 Underline what STDs stand for: Sexually Transmitted Diseases

Scottish Transport Department

2 Underline those infections which affect the genital urinary organs (penis, vagina and reproductive organs).

measles	chlamydia
flu	HIV
gonorrhoea (clap)	chicken pox
syphilis (pox)	acne
whooping cough	warts
herpes	thrush
non-specific urethritis (NSU)	malaria
Hepatitis B	TB

3 Underline the correct answer. STDs can be caught from:

a kissing someone who has one

b toilet seats

c swimming pools

d sharing cups

e having unprotected sex with someone already infected

f shaking hands/touching someone.

4 Underline the correct answer. Men who have STDs:

a rarely have symptoms   **c** sometimes have symptoms
b usually have symptoms   **d** always have symptoms

5 Underline the correct answer. Men who have HIV infection:

a rarely have symptoms   **c** sometimes have symptoms
b usually have symptoms   **d** always have symptoms

NB: Thrush which causes an itchy discharge in women and may cause irritation in men is often not sexually transmitted but could be due to anaemia, pregnancy, taking antibiotics, etc.

Questionnaire • continued •

6 Underline the correct answer. Women who have STDs

    a rarely have symptoms   **c** sometimes have symptoms

    b usually have symptoms   **d** always have symptoms

7 Underline the correct answer. Women who have HIV infection:

    a rarely have symptoms   **c** sometimes have symptoms

    b usually have symptoms   **d** always have symptoms

8 Anyone who is worried they may be HIV positive should go right away for a test. (Delete as appropriate) TRUE / FALSE

9 Some STDs can be fatal. (Delete as appropriate) TRUE / FALSE

10 Some STDs cause infertility in women.
(Delete as appropriate)   TRUE / FALSE

11 Some STDs can cause cervical cancer in women.
(Delete as appropriate)   TRUE / FALSE

12 Some STDs can infect babies.
(Delete as appropriate)   TRUE / FALSE

13 Most STDs can be cured by antibiotics if treated early.
(Delete as appropriate)   TRUE / FALSE

14 Underline the correct answer. STDs are:

    a increasing   **b** decreasing   **c** staying the same.

15 Underline the correct answer. Treatment at a Genito-Urinary clinic is:

    a not confidential   **b** confidential   **c** the GP is told

16 Underline the correct answer. If you have an STD you have a responsibility:

    a to yourself   **b** to yourself and others   **c** to seek help

STD facts

1 STDs stands for sexually transmitted diseases.

2 Infections which affect the genital/urinary organs include:

Gonorrhoea
This causes painful urination and often a discharge from the penis in men.

Often there are no symptoms in women. Sometimes women experience a vaginal discharge and painful urination. If left untreated gonorrhoea is serious: it can often cause pelvic infection and infertility in women so that they cannot have children and it causes blindness in babies through infection during birth.

Chlamydia
A very common and rapidly growing infection. Not much is known about it and it is difficult to detect. It can cause an early morning discharge from the penis in men. Women often have no symptoms. If left untreated Chlamydia is serious: it can often cause pelvic infection and infertility in women so that they cannot have children and it causes eye, ear and throat infection in babies.

HIV (human immunodeficiency virus)
The virus which destroys our immune systems and our ability to fight infection. It survives only in blood, semen and vaginal fluid. You have to have this virus in order to develop AIDS. HIV infection is one of the fastest-growing sexually transmitted diseases and has been found in all parts of the world. Estimates based on available figures suggest that in many countries AIDS may soon become the largest single cause of death of all those in the 20-40 age group. There is no cure for HIV infection or AIDS. Babies can be born with HIV. Usually those with HIV have no symptoms. Broken skin on the genitals caused by other STDs helps spread HIV.

Warts
A common STD. Causes warts on the penis/scrotum and anus in men and on the vulva/vaginal areas and anus in women. Treatment by special lotions is neccessary. Women who have warts must have frequent cervical smear tests since there is a link between warts and cervical cancer.

Herpes
This causes blisters or 'cold sores' on the penis/scrotum or anus in men and on the vulva/vaginal areas or anus in women. Treatment by special drugs is neccessary to make them heal more quickly. There is no cure for herpes. Women with active genital herpes usually have to have babies by Caesarian section. Women who have genital herpes must have frequent cervical smear tests since there is a link between herpes and cervical cancer.

Thrush
Very common. Often caused by pregnancy, the Pill, being on antibiotics, etc. but can sometimes be passed on sexually. Causes an itchy white discharge and soreness around the vaginal and vulval area in women. Treatment by cream or tablets.

NSU (Non-specific urethritis)
Very common. Causes discharge from the penis and pain on passing urine in men. Often no symptoms in women. Treatment is by antibiotics.

Hepatitis B
Caused by a virus transmitted through sexual contact or blood to blood, eg shared needles. Can cause serious liver disease or death. Some carriers may have no symptoms. There is a vaccine which can protect against it. More infectious than HIV.

Syphilis
A serious but now uncommon STD. Causes hard, infectious, painless sores on the genital areas or mouth. Eventually fatal if left untreated. Children born to infected mothers are handicapped. Pregnant women are routinely tested for syphilis.

STD facts – 2

3 STDs in general are caught from intimate bodily contact, although herpes may be spread by active cold sores on the mouth. Some STDs are hard to get, eg HIV, where there has to be an exchange of bodily fluids through penetrative sex.

4 Men who have STDs **sometimes** have symptoms. Things that may worry a man or a woman are pain, lumps, swellings, discharge, sores or blisters. They should seek help from their doctors or from the Genito-urinary Unit at their local hospital.

5 HIV infection **usually causes no symptoms**. It can take from 6 months to 10 years to develop AIDS, ie lose the ability to resist the disease.

6 Women who have STDs **sometimes have symptoms**. This is serious because if left untreated they can:

a develop pelvic infection and become infertile, ie unable to have babies.

b pass on infection during birth to their babies. This means that men must tell their partners about any infection.

7 See 5

8 **False.** This decision needs thinking about carefully. People may not be able to cope with a positive result. Insurance companies discriminate against anyone who has had a test. Sometimes people do not react with sympathy. Anyone who is considering having a test should first ring a counselling service such as Aidsline in order to talk this over.

9 **True** – Some STDs can be fatal, eg HIV and Syphilis

10 **True** – See 6 above

11 **True** – Cervical cancer is linked to Genital Warts and other factors such as smoking, occupation, personal hygiene and whether condoms are used. Cervical cancer is on the increase – women who are sexually active are recommended to have a check-up every three years.

12 **True.** Gonorrhoea causes blindness. Syphilis causes handicap. HIV can cause illness and death.

13 **True.** Most STDs are treatable. Some have no cure, eg HIV and herpes.

14 **STDs are increasing**. The most dramatic increase is in HIV. Although there is some evidence that the rate of new infection in homosexual men is decreasing, new infection amongst heterosexual men and women is increasing rapidly and is recognised as a major health problem in most countries in the world.

Chlamydia and cervical cancer are also increasing, especially among young women. The increase in Gonorrhoea is worrying because it shows that some people continue to risk unsafe sex.

15 Treatment at a Genito-Urinary clinic is **confidential** but people will be given help as to how to discuss it with their partners.

16 All three apply if a person has STDs.

STDs

In twos examine these situations and answer the questions.

1 Someone has an active cold sore (herpes) on his/her lip. What should he/she do?

....

....

....

2 Someone has a discharge from his penis. What should he do?

....

....

....

3 Someone has thrush and in spite of using cream from the doctor it keeps coming back. What should she/he do?

....

....

....

4 Someone has gone to the Genito-Urinary clinic and has found that he/she has gonorrhoea. What should he/she do?

....

....

....

5 In the past, someone had unprotected sex. Now, he/she is in a stable sexual relationship. Is there anything to worry about and if so, what should he/she do?

....

....

....

STDs – values continuum

In groups of five or six write out your values continuum statements and place them on the table. One end of the table is marked as **agree**, one as **disagree**. In turn each of you should take a statement, read it out and place it on the table to show your opinion. Others in your group are then free to pick up any statement and move it around the table where they think fit, as long as they explain why they are doing this.

Values Continuum Statements

Which of these statements do you think will be most true in five years?

AGREE	DISAGREE
There is no risk of anyone like me in my culture getting an STD.	The problem of STDs / HIV is bound to increase.
Whatever the Government says people won't use condoms anyway.	I think young people will be more careful about choosing sexual partners.
People will become less embarrassed about seeking help.	I think young people would be too scared to go to a GU clinic.
The cases of STDs / HIV will be going down because people will be using safer sex.	We'll be able to discuss these things with our partners.

Health and welfare case studies • 1 •

Sharon has just discovered, to her horror, that a former boyfriend is now injecting drugs. She has started a new relationship with Dave.

Why do you think she is worried?
Advice now to Sharon and Dave . . .

Would your advice protect this couple's health and welfare?

With two small children to look after, Parveen and Shafiq are feeling pretty run down. Parveen has one cold after another and can't seem to shake them off. They don't think Parveen could cope with another pregnancy right now. They are both Muslim. Do you think Parveen and Shafiq should consider using contraception?
If not, why not?

If so, what methods do your think they should consider?

Ron is 17 and boasts a lot about the number of girls he has had sex with. He's not afraid of AIDS or getting a girl pregnant and says it's up to girls to sort that out.
Your reactions to Ron . . .

Advice now to any girl Ron meets . . .

Health and welfare case studies • 2 •

Eric knows that he is HIV positive. He has fallen in love with Mandy. He is very worried that if he tells her he is infectious, she will end the relationship.
Advice now to Eric . . .

If the relationship continued, should they ever consider having children?

Sue got drunk at a party last night and ended up having sex with someone she met there. They took no precautions.
Advice now to Sue . . .

List the risks that Sue took:

Lisa is 17 and feels sure that she is lesbian but so far has had no relationships. She is attracted to somebody who she feels sure feels the same way.
Advice now to Lisa . . .

Are lesbians more at risk from AIDS than heterosexuals?

Health and welfare case studies · 3 ·

Dave and Linda have been going out with each other since they left school. Dave wants to have sex with Linda but Linda is not sure. When she asks Dave about condoms he says they can think about that later. Why do you think Linda is worried?

Comment on Dave's attitude:

Advice now to Dave and Linda . . .

Alex is 17 and feels sure that he is gay but so far has had no relationships. He is attracted to somebody who he feels sure feels the same way. Advice now to Alex . . .

Are gay men more at risk from AIDS than heterosexuals?

Sean and Theresa have a four-month-old baby. They do not want another child yet. They are practising Catholics.
Do you think they should consider using contraception?

If not, why not?

If so, what method/s would you advise and why?

Health and welfare case studies • 4 •

Maria and Tony have just got married. Both have been married before. They now have three children, two from Maria's previous marriage and one from Tony's. Tony is sure he doesn't want any more children. Maria doesn't want to make her mind up just yet.

Advice now to Maria and Tony regarding:

a contraception

b health

Ahmed and Rizwana are getting married soon. They are both happy about this but Rizwana is worried. Someone has told her that, although he has settled down now, Ahmed used to hang around with quite a wild bunch of friends.

Why do you think Rizwana is worried?

Do you think she should raise her worries with a) Ahmed, b) anyone else?

Advice now to this couple . . .

Attitudes quiz

Test your own attitudes by underlining the ones you most identify with. Then check with someone you trust to see if they think you have the kind of attitudes which will protect your health and welfare in the future.

How safe is this attitude? safe ⟶ unsafe

1 'People with infectious diseases should be locked up and then the rest of us would be safe.'_____

2 'I think it's important to be open with a partner about any previous sexual experiences.'_____

3 'As long as I stick to one partner I'll be all right.'_____

4 'I shall always put my own health first, no matter what my partner may say.'_____

5 'Men should wear condoms when having sex.'_____

6 'You need to use condoms for a few months till you are really sure about your relationship - then go on the Pill.'_____

7 'I'd be really embarassed to carry condoms.'_____

8 'I prefer to be celibate.'_____

9 'We shouldn't just assume that our partners tell us everything.'_____

10 'If people are mature enough to make a relationship sexual they should be mature enough to talk about health and contraception beforehand.'_____

Coping with pressure

Objectives

To provide students with the opportunity:

1 to define the meaning and effects of stress, including positive and negative aspects

2 to identify situations which may cause individuals stress

3 to become aware of external factors which influence the level of stress

4 to explore different ways of reducing stress

5 to recognise moments of stress in their own lives

6 to identify different ways of coping with stress in the short term

7 to practise relaxation methods.

Methodology

Lesson 1 and Lesson 2

After a brainstorming session, students complete *student booklet* activity in pairs. They compare their answers with the information sheet. An individual activity is followed by a class discussion. Groups then complete the *student booklet* activity after playing the *Potential stress situations* card game. Whole class feedback completes the lesson. This may take two lessons.

Lesson 3

Ask students to relate how they cope with stressful situations, and what stressful situations they have had. Students should discuss coping strategies in pairs, and a class list should be compiled from feedback. A practical relaxation situation could follow.

Resources

Potential stress situations cards	106
Teachers' notes on relaxation	109
Student Booklet (1 per student)	111
Phone directory/Thomson's directory	
A spacious room where students can relax on their backs	

Coping with pressure

1 Brainstorm the word **stress**. What comes into your mind when you think of the word? Record.

2 Students should refer to *student booklet* page 1 *Stress performance curve* and then turn to *student booklet* page 2, *Stressful situations for students*.

3 In pairs, students rank those situations which they consider most stressful. They should then compare their answers with the definitive list on *student booklet* page 3 *Stress what is it?*

4 Students as individuals complete *student booklet* page 4 *Individual stress*. Make clear to students that this is for their information only.

5 Ask for a show of hands to determine level of stress within the class. Who thinks they suffer symptoms of stress:

- never?
- sometimes?
- often?
- most of the time?
- all the time?

Teacher note:

Although *student booklet* page 4 *Individual Stress*, is confidential, a teacher may become aware of students who are suffering from severe stress. These students should be supported by the teacher or given an opportunity to see someone else in school and/or another agency. One of the best ways of relieving stress in the short term is to talk to someone.

6 In groups read the statements on the *Potential stress situation cards*. Place each card under the heading 'Within your control', 'Not sure' or 'More difficult to control'. Discuss each one briefly before placing the card.

7 Look at the cards under the heading 'Within your control'. Ask each group to make a list of the ways in which they think these areas could be reduced or eliminated. They should record their answers on *student booklet* page 5.

8 Look at the example at the bottom of the page. Each group should look at the cards they placed under the heading 'More difficult to control'. Is it difficult to decide what action to take when we look at these? They should record three situations where they agree that it is hard to decide what to do.

9 Whole class feedback on activities. Try to extract the key ways of dealing with stress.

Lesson 3
Dealing with stress

1 Refer back to *student booklet* page 4 *Individual stress*. Ask students if they have any of these stress reactions. If so how do they cope with them? Brainstorm coping methods and record on the blackboard.

(Be ready for negative as well as positive responses and be ready to deal with the implications of negative choices – eg use of drugs/alcohol).

2 Ask students to think about four or five situations over the past few months which have caused them concern or stress:

- mock exams
- Records of Achievement
- not getting a work experience placement
- being fed up in school
- pressure from parents
- course work deadlines
- interviews
- planning for a future career
- applying for a college place or job.

Students discuss in pairs how they can relieve pressure for themselves.

3 From group feedback compile a list of strategies. Add any strategies from the list below which have been omitted.

- **personal organisation** eg such as organisation of time, setting deadlines, asking for help such as asking other people to take on your responsibilities at home for a short time while you revise
- **altering the physical environment** eg no bells between lessons, carpets in classrooms, ask for TV off when you are doing your work
- **relaxation**
- **seeking emotional support** eg seeking help from friends, family, teacher or other agencies

4 Practical session – see *teachers' notes* on page 109.

Practical session – see *teachers' notes* on page 109.

Extension task
Agencies which help us

In class brainstorm agencies which may offer support. List them. Look in the phone directory, Thomson's Directory and information from your Community Health Council for further ideas. Students should select an agency which interests them, perhaps they could agree in the class to take a different one each. Students write to the agency requesting information, eg who they help, opening hours, where they are, do they run a help line, etc. Students should explain in their letters that they are writing a guide for young people on 'Agencies Which Help Us' This could be done as homework. The compiling of the booklet could be a group or class task.

NOTES

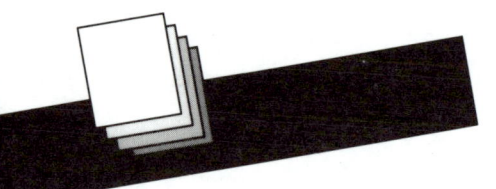

Potential stress situations

Instructions

These pages should be photocopied, one set for each group, cut up and stuck on to cardboard. Do the same with the instructions and keep with each set of cards.

Cut up these boxes and place them on your group's table. Put the headings **Within your control**, **More difficult to control**, and **Not sure** at the top. Take turns to read each card and then place each card under a heading after your group has discussed where it should go.

Within your control

More difficult to control

Not sure

On the morning of your exam your alarm clock doesn't go off and you oversleep.

You have forgotten your homework, again.

Someone has borrowed your coursework. Your teacher wants to mark it but your friend has not returned it.

A teacher constantly rings your parent or guardian.

The family has been unable to keep up the payments on their house and is threatened with eviction.

Your eldest brother has not paid his council tax and faces a court case or prison.

For moral reasons you decide you want to become a vegetarian. This causes problems within your family.

You are expected to work long hours in the family business at the expense of school work.

Someone calls you a racist name.

Someone bullies you.

Someone in your class constantly disrupts lessons and you can't get on with your work.

You have revised for a test and the teacher is absent.

A difference arises between a group of friends and you are left out.

You are told off for being late. The reason you are late is that your teacher over-ran the previous lesson.

Coursework deadlines are drawing near and it is impossible for you to get the work in on time.

Being the eldest, you are expected to look after younger children and have to take time off school.

Your parents are planning to separate.

At the end of the school day you have to change a pair of expensive trainers which are damaged. You have no receipt, but would like a new pair.

Potential stress situations ·continued·

You hear screams from next door most nights. You think the child is being hit.	Your parent is made redundant.
You have nowhere quiet to do your homework at home.	You are looking forward to watching a programme and someone else wants to watch another channel.
Parents insist you visit relatives when you want to do your work at the weekend.	Your family is being harassed by a local teenager.
You can't sleep because you are worried abut the test tomorrow.	It is painful when you go to the toilet and you have to go to your doctor to discuss it.
A close relative suddenly dies.	You have to care for a sick parent.
You can't do your homework because you have to cook the meal.	

Dealing with stress

Most people are far from relaxed. We often tense muscles out of habit and are unaware of the resulting tension. The aim of these techniques is to introduce to students the skills of muscle relaxation and mental quieting which will lead them to feel more in control of their feelings. The result of successful relaxation is to regulate rapid heart rate, uneven breathing, increased sweating, dry mouth, churning stomach and other sensations related to anxiety. Many people use relaxation techniques, eg top athletes, chess grand masters, etc. It is quite normal and not odd!

The aim should be to use relaxation techniques automatically and unselfconsciously whenever the need arises. Remember, the more you practise, the easier it becomes.

Relaxation techniques

1   *Relaxing where you are*. Sit on your chairs with your feet on the ground. Lean forward so that your elbows rest firmly on your knees. Lean forwards slightly. Let your hands hang loose and your head drop forward.

    or

2   Lean forward on to your desk. Keep your fingers relaxed. Keep your feet flat on the ground. Let your head rest on your arms or your hands.

    Which position, one or two, do you find most comfortable? Get into that position now.

3   *Breathing to relax*. Breathe calmly. Breathe in deeply and breathe out slowly, six to ten breaths a minute. When we are upset we breathe fast. Sixteen or more breaths a minute can lead to hyperventilation (overbreathing) which makes you feel worried and strange.

    Keep your body relaxed as you breathe in and out. Keep breathing slowly for a few minutes.

4   *Mental quieting*. Say firmly to yourself **Stop** (worrying, fussing, shouting, etc). Take a breath in and then breathe out slowly. Relax your shoulders and hands. Talk to yourself again. 'I feel calm. There is no need to worry.' Take another breath and as you breathe out relax your lips and jaw. Repeat and talk to yourself again.

5   *Hand relaxation*. Clench your hands and fists tight. Now shake your hands loose, stretching your fingers. Rest your hands in a comfortable position, in your lap or on the desk top. Can you feel the tension being released when you shake your hands?

6   *Shoulder relaxation*. Tighten your shoulders slightly, then release. Shrug your shoulders up and down. Wriggle them until they feel relaxed. Let your shoulders drop as low as they can, then relax.

7   *Deep relaxation*. Sit comfortably in a chair or lie down if preferred. Close your eyes. Calm your mind. Breathe slowly. Let your breath out gently. Breathe gently in and out. Feel your back relax into the chair or on to the floor.

Start at your feet. Tense them, then relax. Tense them, then relax. Now your ankles. Tense them, then relax. Tense them, then relax. Now your knees. Tense them, then relax. Tense them, then relax.

Feel the tension coming out as you breathe out.

Now your thighs. Tense them, then relax. Tense them, then relax.

If your mind wanders, say to yourself, 'relax, calm'.

Now your stomach muscles. Tense them, then relax. Tense them, then relax. Now your chest muscles. Tense them, then relax. Tense them, then relax. Now your fingers. Tense them, then relax. Tense them, then relax. Now your elbows. Tense them, then relax. Tense them, then relax. Now your shoulders. Tense them, then relax. Tense them, then relax. Now open your mouth wide, relax. Open, then relax. Now frown your forehead. Tense it, then relax. Tense it then relax.

Take in a deep breath. Blow out. Open your eyes. Get up slowly and shake yourself.

NOTES

Personal & Social Education
and cross-curricular themes

Student Booklet

Term 2 Module 5

Coping with pressure

name

form   date

Stress performance curve

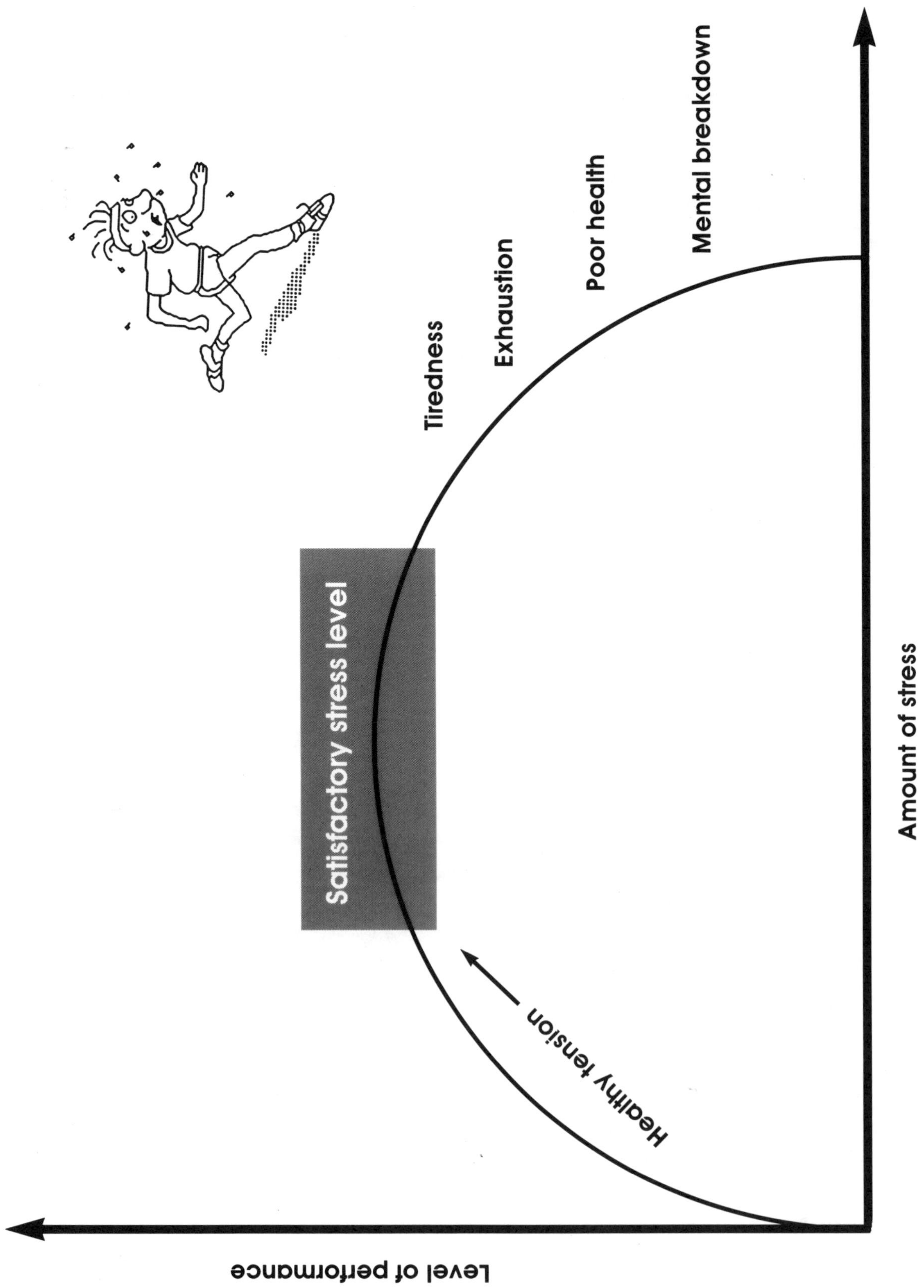

Tiredness

Exhaustion

Poor health

Mental breakdown

Satisfactory stress level

Healthy tension

Amount of stress

Level of performance

Stressful situations for students

Look at the list below of possible stressful situations young people may come across. Rank them in order of importance, writing in the most stressful at the top.

We think the most stressful are. . .

Lack of privacy

Concern about appearance, weight or identity

Conflict with parents

Difficulty in making decisions

General feelings of frustration

Death of a parent

In trouble with the law

Interviews or starting a new job

Sexual difficulties

Not part of the crowd

Death of a close friend

Serious health problems eg surgery

School pressures, exams, deadlines

Recent move, home, school, college

Parents having rows or in financial trouble

Engagement or marriage

Insecurity about future

Loss of a parent through divorce

Break up with boy or girl friend

Unemployed, financial trouble

Driving test

Death of a close relative

Stress – what is it?

Current thinking shows that young people find the following situations stressful. The list begins with the most stressful. If people experience too many of these changes over a short time, they are more likely to become ill, either physically or mentally. The dictionary definition of stress is . . . stress, n. strain: pressure: force.

Death of a parent
Death of a close relative
Loss of a parent through divorce
Death of a close friend
Parents having rows or in financial trouble
Serious health problems – surgery/pregnancy
Engagement or marriage
Conflict with parents
In trouble with the law
Unemployed, financial trouble
Break up with boy or girl friend
Interviews or starting a new job
Insecurity about future
Sexual difficulties
Not part of the crowd
Lack of privacy
Driving test
School pressures, exams, deadlines
Difficulty in making decisions
Concern about appearance, weight or identity
Recent move, home, school, college
General feelings of frustration

A certain amount of stress is beneficial for us. People need stress in order to perform well, eg a tennis player before a big match (see *Stress performance curve*) or a student before an exam.

Everyone has a different stress level where they perform well but going beyond that level of stress will lead to problems, eg tension, exhaustion, concentration and memory problems, anger, anxiety, depression or ill-health.

Industry is severely affected by stress-related illnesses. One recent estimate has put the total cost of stress to industry at £28 billion a year in terms of lost hours, accidents and sub-standard work.

As we have seen, stress is normal and a certain amount can have positive effects. But when excessive stress occurs it is important to *recognise* it and *deal with it*.

You can deal with it by relaxation or by changing the situation which is causing it or by seeking help.

Individual stress

Find out how stressed you are by filling in this questionnaire.
Don't show the results to anyone else.

Do you ever	never	sometimes	often	most of the time	all of the time
sleep badly					
feel moody					
get headaches					
find it difficult to concentrate					
get anxious					
feel irritable					
take days off school					
feel depressed					
lose your sense of humour					
feel things are your fault					
have difficulty concentrating					
get physically tense					
feel ill					
overeat or lose your appetite					
feel you don't care about anything					
get annoyed with your family or friends					
feel unable to cope					
lose your self-confidence					
get angry					
stop seeing your friends					
Total ticks					

If you have a lot of ticks in the last three columns you may be living with more stress than is good for you. Find out about some ways of reducing your stress.

Potential stress situations

Look at the cards you have placed under the heading 'within your control'. Record below the ways in which your group felt these causes of stress could be reduced or eliminated.

Look at the cards you have placed under the heading 'more difficult to control'. Choose three situations your group wants to look at in more depth. These should be situations where it is difficult to decide what action to take. Below we provide a similar example and possible ways of thinking about it. Complete the column 'Which is the best choice?'. Then write in your own three situations on the next page and analyse them in the same way, completing all the columns.

Example	*Why might it be difficult to decide on a plan of action?*	*List the possible courses of action you could take*	*Which is the best choice?*
A parent of yours is becoming increasingly violent to the family at home	1 Interferes with privacy of family. 2 Could bring shame upon family. 3 Could break up the family. 4 Things could get worse and you are dependent on the family. 5 You are not sure who to turn to. 6 This is something totally new and you don't know anyone else who has had this experience. 7 You love your parent.	1 Talk to the parent who is being violent. 2 Consider your behaviour and make sure you avoid confrontation. 3 Talk to someone else in the family. 4 Talk to someone outside your family, eg doctor/teacher/neighbour/community leader. 5 Run away from home. 6 Call the police. 7 Remove all the family to a family refuge centre.	

Potential stress situations • continued •

	Why might it be difficult to decide on a plan of action?	List the possible courses of action you could take	Which is the best choice?
Situation 1			
Situation 2			
Situation 3			

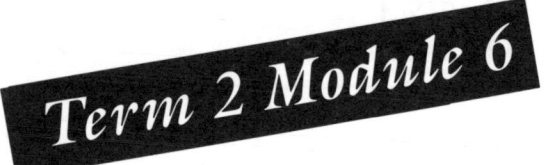

Drugs and health

Objectives

To provide students with the opportunity:

1 to increase critical awareness of prescribed and over the counter drugs

2 to practise explaining clearly what their health problem is to their doctors

3 to understand any advice given and to ask for and get clarification where necessary

4 to gain knowledge about common forms of medication

5 to increase awareness of the risks of not following instructions about drugs

6 to gain knowledge through research about different alternative forms of treatment

7 to increase critical awareness of claims about alternative treatments and therapies.

Methodology

Lesson 1 and Lesson 2 After introduction students play *card sort* game in groups. In groups students role play the scenarios, which are followed by a whole class discussion. Students play *options and consequences* game in groups

Lesson 3 and Lesson 4 Introduce topic to students and give them suggestions for research topics, research methods and presentation methods. Students undertake research in pairs and present research to the class.

Resources

Teachers' Note on recommended resources	121
Card sort (1 set for each group)	122
Student Booklet (1 per student)	127

Telephone directory/Thomson's directory

Any local information available on drug agencies and alternative therapies, eg from Community Health Council and local Health Promotion Unit, should be collected in advance. Resources could be placed in school library or resource base if more independent research skills are to be encouraged.

Drugs and health

Lesson 1 and 2 "Doctor, doctor"

1 Emphasise the following points in the introduction:

• You are either sixteen or almost sixteen. At this age you have the right to go to your doctor and ask for confidential advice and treatment. You can give consent to your own treatment, eg if you need an operation. You may be given drugs on prescription

• This means your health is now in your hands. You are responsible, not anyone else. If you don't ask the right questions about your treatment no-one else is going to do it for you. You need to know about and understand what you are putting into your own body. You need to arm yourself with knowledge so that your needs are met.

• Drugs can affect your body in powerful ways. If misused they can be very dangerous. It is believed that more people in Britain are killed each year by prescribed drugs than by accidents on the roads. The purpose of this unit is to make you more skilled and confident to ask the right questions about all sorts of drugs and treatments.

2 Distribute one set of *card sort* cards to each group of four. Students must match the front and the back of the cards, ie the name of the drug with the suppliers. Groups should discuss their choices. Move around and assist groups as required. Students may like to test each other at the end of the lesson.

Correct answers are: **1** Antibiotics **B**   **2** Antiseptics **C**   **3** Decongestant **G**
4 Anti-anxiety drugs **J**   **5** Anti-depressants **A**   **6** Anti-histamine **D**
7 Antacid **E**   **8** Analgesic **H**   **9** Steroids **F**   **10** Topical **I**

3 Invite students to reflect on how they feel as they walk into a doctor's surgery, using the introduction to *student booklet* page 1 as a prompt. Nervous? Anxious? Lots of people find it hard to make the most of their time with the doctor. Although doctors are trained to be very knowledgeable about illness and its treatment, there is one thing you know more about than they do and that is how you feel: what exactly has made you concerned enough about your health to make an appointment? You need to explain this as clearly as possible if you want the doctor to do his/her job. You then need to make sure that you understand the doctor's advice; ask further questions if you are not clear. The role plays are designed to let you practise being clear and confident.

4 Students work in groups of four on the two scenarios on *student booklet* pages 1-4. Each group should do both, each person in the group reading a part. Groups analyse the behaviours of the characters, answer the questions on the worksheet and then re-write the scripts with the patients taking a more assertive role. Groups perform the new scripts.

5 Class discussion – What are the questions we should ask when we go to the doctor's? What are the potential risks of not following instructions?

6 Look at *student booklet* page 5. Students add any further points they would find it useful to remember.

7 Students check their own understanding of prescribed drugs by working in groups on *student booklet* page 6 *Options and consequences*. They should then check their answers on *student booklet* page 7.

Lesson 3 and 4
What are the alternatives?

1 Clarify patients' rights to NHS treatment, using *student booklet* page 8 *What are the alternatives?* as background. Introduce subject of alternative or complimentary treatments. Some are offered by qualified doctors.

2 Using *student booklet* page 9 as a briefing, explain that there are a host of alternative approaches. How could you know if they were worth trying? Could any do more harm than good? Are they just an expensive rip-off? How would you find a good practitioner, if you were interested? Ask class if anyone has personal experience of such approaches. Introduce *student booklet* page 10, *Complementary medicines*. Explain the selection of research topics available. Ask pairs to volunteer to take a project. Cover as many as possible. Contract with each pair to produce a presentation on their topic. Give them a realistic time limit. Allocate wall space and presentation materials if desired.

Research methods to be encouraged might include: going to the school library and local library, looking in the phone book and writing to organisations for information, asking family and friends about personal experiences, checking whether practitioners advertise in local paper.

Methods of presentation might include:

speech

article

question and answer session

taped report

poster.

Extra credit could be given to those who use local information and services (Local Community Health Councils and Yellow Pages are a good source.)

3 Support students in their research from a selection of the following topics:

Hypnotherapy
Osteopathy
Naturopathy
Homeopathy
Acupuncture
Aromatherapy
Reflexology
Herbalism

4 Students present findings. Class should distill main messages about any sort of the treatment which is offered.

NOTES

Drug education in year 11

In earlier sections of the programme, we have studied the risks of drug use, both legal and illegal, through giving pupils the opportunity to use action research methods. These risks have included the physical, emotional, and psychological effects of drugs and also associated risks, eg HIV/AIDS. The programme has tried to be informative rather than to use 'scare tactics'.

This particular module concentrates on prescribed drugs, an area often ignored in other drugs packs. This area is relevant to all young people, especially at this age when they become legally responsible for consenting to treatment. The module is approached from the point of view of the consumer.

Sometimes our year 11 pupils request further drug education because of local issues that arise from their neighbourhood's sub-culture on drugs. When that happens we try to make a response tailored to the needs of the particular year group at the time, drawing on briefings to pastoral staff from our local community drugs teams and voluntary agencies.

Resources we have found useful to draw on include:

Taking Drugs Seriously – A Manual Of Harm Reduction Education On Drugs, by Ian Clements, Julian Cohen and James Kay, published 1990 by Healthwise Helpline Ltd, 4th Floor, 10-12 James St, Liverpool L2 7PQ

Drugnotes published by Institutes of the Study for Drug Dependancy (ISDD)

Drugwise published by ISDD/TACADE/LIFESKILLS,1986

1 **ANTIBIOTICS** *FACT CARD*	**2** **ANTISEPTICS** *FACT CARD*
3 **DECONGESTANT** *FACT CARD*	**4** **ANTI-ANXIETY DRUGS** *FACT CARD*
5 **ANTIDEPRESSANTS** *FACT CARD*	**6** **ANTI-HISTAMINE** *FACT CARD*

Card sort

J   DETAILS

- These are called relaxants or tranquillisers.
- At a lower dose they calm you down, act as a 'sedative'.
- At a higher dose they send you to sleep, act as a 'hypnotic'.
- A common sort, the benzodiazepines, are habit-forming and should only be taken for a short period of time. They have side-effects and can affect the ability to drive or operate machinery.

  In the past many people were prescribed these and addiction is a common problem.

H   DETAILS

- Pain-relieving drugs for mild to moderate pain: aspirin and paracetamol.
- For moderate pain: ibuprofen.
- For severe pain control morphine and morphine-related medicines can be prescribed. These have side effects such as constipation and can be habit-forming.

  Aspirin should be avoided by those with stomach problems. Many people with a history of asthma are allergic to aspirin.

  It is dangerous to take more than the recommended dose of any of them.

A   DETAILS

- Treat the symptoms felt by people who are very depressed, but do not deal with the cause of depression.
- One sort, the mono-amino oxidise inhibitor drugs (MAOI), are dangerous if taken with certain foods so a strict diet advised by the doctor must be followed.
- Can have a variety of side effects.

F   DETAILS

- Drugs similar to the hormones produced by your body in the adrenal gland.
- Can be used against allergies or asthma.
- Can be used against pain or inflammation in the joints.
- If taking corticosteroid tablets you must carry a card with you at all times and show it to doctors, nurses and dentists every time you are treated.
- You must never just stop taking them (very dangerous) unless your doctor knows.
- After-effects can last up to several years.
- Found in several skin creams; relieves symptoms but can make skin thinner.

D   DETAILS

- Act to reduce the body's reaction in case of allergy, eg hay fever.
- Can be in tablets, creams or cold medicines.
- If they cause drowsiness, do not drive or operate machinery.
- Can in themselves cause allergic reactions and should not be used for long periods.
- Found in skin creams such as Anthisan and Wasp-Eze.
- Found in Actifed, Benylin, Night Nurse and lots of other cold medicines.

E   DETAILS

- Are often taken to relieve the discomfort of indigestion or ulcers.
- They neutralise stomach acids and this stops the pain.
- Tell your doctor what you are taking for your indigestion if he/she proposes to prescribe you a medicine for something else. Antacids affect the way your stomach absorb things and should not be taken for a long time without your doctor knowing.
- Some act as laxatives and some make you constipated.

Card sort

B DETAILS

- Very useful for infections caused by bacteria.
- Useless against viruses.
- Some people are allergic to one of the commonest antibiotics: penicillin. They must not take it. It could kill them.
- Must be used long enough to kill each bacterium, otherwise the bacterium adapts and becomes resistant to that antibiotic. This is why you must finish taking all the medicine even if you feel better.

C DETAILS

- Used to kill or prevent the growth of an organism on the surface of the body, eg the skin. Sometimes called germicides. Found in creams and lotions.

G DETAILS

- Used to unblock nasal, sinal or bronchial passages so that you can breathe more easily.
- One sort, the sympathomimetics, relax bronchial muscles. These are found in lots of over the counter cold medicines, eg Actifed, Lemsip, Sudafed. People with high blood pressure, heart disease or diabetes shouldn't take them without their doctor's knowledge.
- Lozenges and linctuses help to relieve sore throats.
- Expectorants make phlegm more watery.

I DETAILS

- A medicine applied directly to the skin, eyes or ears, never lick or swallow it!
- Could be a cream, lotion or powder.
- Must never be given to a friend, skin is sensitive and this could cause itching, rashes or allergies.
- Depending on what it is prescribed for, could contain antibiotics, anti-fungal drugs, antihistamines, antiseptics, corticosteroids, local anaesthetics, etc.
- Sometimes says 'For External Use Only'.
- Should not be kept in cupboard for longer than time limit.

Card sort

7	8
ANTACID	**ANALGESIC**
FACT CARD	*FACT CARD*

9	10
STEROID	**TOPICAL**
FACT CARD	*FACT CARD*

Personal & Social Education
and cross-curricular themes

Student Booklet

Term 2 Module 6

Drugs and health

name

form   date

Role plays

You are either sixteen or almost sixteen. At this age you have the right to go to the doctor and ask for confidential advice and treatment. You can give consent to your own treatment, eg if you need an operation. You may be given drugs on prescription. This means your health is now in your hands. You are responsible, no-one else. If you don't ask the right questions about your treatment no-one else is going to do it for you. You need to know about and understand what you are putting into your own body. You need to arm yourself with knowledge so that your needs are met.

Did you know?

Drugs can affect your body in powerful ways. Eighteen per cent of men and twenty eight per cent of women are regularly taking some form of medication prescribed by a doctor. Four out of five visits to the doctor end with the writing of a prescription.

If misused drugs can be very dangerous. It is believed that more people in Britain are killed each year by prescribed drugs than by accidents on the roads. The purpose of this module is to make you more skilled and confident to ask the right questions about all sorts of drugs and treatments.

DOCTOR, DOCTOR

How do you feel as you walk into a doctor's surgery? Nervous? Anxious? Lots of people find it hard to make the most of their time with the doctor. Although doctors are trained to be very knowledgeable about illness and its treatment there is one thing you know more about than they do and that is how you feel, what exactly has made you concerned enough about your health to make an appointment. You need to explain this as clearly as possible if you want the doctor to do his/her job. You then need to make sure that you understand the doctor's advice, asking further questions if you are not clear. The role plays are designed to let you practise being clear and confident.

Work in groups of four and read through Role play 1 and Role play 2, so that you each read a part. Change Mr Jones to Ms Jones or your own name if appropriate.

When you have discussed the questions in the boxes at the bottom of each page, read the information on the next page.

Note here any information you want the patient to give, and any questions he/she should ask the doctor.

Rewrite the script with the patient taking a more assertive role.

Role play 1

**Doctor writing at desk . . .
there is a knock on the door**

Doctor	Come in.
Patient	(enters room hesitantly)
Doctor	(without looking up) Sit down.
Patient	Er, good morning Doctor.
Doctor	(continues to write)
Patient	(looks increasingly nervous) Erm, I've had a problem with my back.
Doctor	(without looking up) Mr Jones is it?
Patient	(smiling faintly) Yes Doctor.
Doctor	Well, what's the trouble Mr Jones?
Patient	Well, I've had a bad back ache over the past ...
Doctor	Back eh? (looks up briefly)
Patient	Yes, you see ...
Doctor	Right, take one of these three times a day. (starts to write out prescription)
Patient	Oh right. When should I ...
Doctor	Right, that should help. Good day. (hands over prescription and continues to write on note-pad)
Patient	(uncertainly) Well, thank you Doctor. (leaves room)

Discuss amongst yourselves

Was this a useful appointment? How did the doctor behave? What was his/her tone of voice? How would the doctor's body language affect the patient? How would the layout of the room affect the patient? What do you think the patient expected to happen?

Role play 2

**Doctor writing at desk . . .
there is a knock on the door**

Doctor	Come in.
Patient	(enters room hesitantly)
Doctor	(looking up and smiling) Do take a seat.
Patient	Good morning Doctor.
Doctor	Good morning. Mr Jones isn't it?
Patient	Yes Doctor.
Doctor	Now, what seems to be the trouble?
Patient	Well doctor, I've had trouble with my back.
Doctor	Oh dear. When did this start?
Patient	Well, a few days ago.
Doctor	Where exactly does it hurt?
Patient	(indicates spot in small of the back) I've been decorating recently. It may have been caused by that.
Doctor	Very possibly. Not to worry. We'll soon sort it out.
Patient	Well, what exactly do you think I've done?
Doctor	You've probably just pulled a muscle. I'll give you a prescription. (starts to write)
Patient	What treatment are you giving me?
Doctor	Oh, just something to take the pain away.
Patient	I prefer not to have any sort of sedative.
Doctor	Don't worry Mr Jones. This will sort you out. (hands over prescription.)
Patient	Well .... (takes prescription but seems worried) ..... erm ....
Doctor	Right. Goodbye Mr Jones.
Patient	Oh. Good bye Doctor. (leaves room)

—— Discuss amongst yourselves ——

Was this any better? How was it different from the first scenario? In what ways might the patient still be unhappy about the interview?

Role play 3

Doctor writing at desk . . .
there is a knock on the door

Doctor

Patient

Doctor

Patient

Doctor

Patient

Doctor

Patient

Doctor

Patient

Doctor

Patient

Doctor

Patient

Doctor

Patient

Doctor

Patient

Doctor

Patient

Main messages

I'd like an appointment please

You have the right to see a doctor at your GP's surgery at any time during surgery hours. If there is an appointment system you could be given one for a later surgery as long as the delay wouldn't risk your health. The receptionist is there to ensure access to the doctor. You don't need to give details of your symptoms to the receptionist. If you know you will need an examination you could mention it, some doctors allow longer appointments for this.

It's OK

You are entitled to seek help and feel that you have had a decent service. When you come out of the surgery you should feel that:

- you were listened to and understood
- you made the most of your time with the doctor
- you gave clear information
- you understand the advice you were given
- if given a prescription you know how to use the medicine safely and effectively.

But . . . I'm still not better

Go back and explain this, eg

- if your medicine doesn't work or has effects you weren't expecting
- if you don't understand what is wrong with you and are worried
- if you would like a second opinion about what is wrong with you
- if you don't understand the advice you were given
- if you are feeling worse or have developed new symptoms.

Do	Don't
<ul><li>find out the name of the medicine</li><li>ask what it is for</li><li>ask if there are foods, drinks or other medicines you should avoid while taking it</li><li>ask when you should take it, how often and how many at a time</li><li>ask how long you should continue taking it</li><li>ask if there are any side-effects you should know about</li><li>ask if there are things not to do, eg driving or operating machinery</li><li>ask what you should do if you miss a dose</li><li>report any side effects</li><li>tell the doctor of any allergies to medicines</li><li>tell the doctor if you are already taking some medicines</li></ul>	<ul><li>delay once you realise you need medical help: make an appointment</li><li>be put off by the mystique of the doctor, tell him/her exactly how you are feeling</li><li>leave the surgery if you are not clear about the advice or treatment you have been given; write it down if necessary</li><li>ignore the instructions on the bottle</li><li>forget what you have taken, get a little box and put the correct dosage for the day in it if you know you are forgetful</li><li>let anyone else use medicines prescribed for you</li><li>keep old medicines in the cupboard, they can lose their effect or actually become harmful</li></ul>

Options and consequences

1 You've been sick after three tablets. Do you:

a   Carry on taking them despite your sickness.

b   Stop taking them and hope you get better.

c   Contact your doctor and explain the problem.

2 You can't remember how many antibiotic tablets you've taken today. Do you:

a   Play safe and take another.

b   Assume you've taken enough and continue the course.

c   Think 'Oh, I've missed one now. I might as well stop'.

3 You go down with what you think is the same bug your sister has just had. Do you:

a   Help yourself to her left-over medicine.

b   Make an appointment for yourself at the doctor's.

c   Do nothing.

4 You are feeling down and fed up. Someone offers you a 'pick me up'. Do you:

a   Say 'no thanks. I don't like taking pills.'

b   Say 'right-oh then'.

c   Take it because you don't want to offend them.

5 Your skin is very sore. There is some cream in the medicine cabinet. Do you:

a   Use it.

b   Go to your doctor or pharmacist and explain your symptoms.

c   Read the instructions carefully and check the sell-by date.

6 You have been prescribed something but then hear something about it on TV that concerns you. Do you:

a   Assume it's scaremongering and continue to take it.

b   Throw it in the bin.

c   Go back and ask your doctor about it.

7 Your eye is very sore. You see some suitable-looking drops in the medicine cabinet. Do you:

a   Think 'Never use someone else's medicine' and go to ask the pharmacist's advice.

b   Use them.

c   Look at the sell-by date, check the seal, if opened check how long they have been open, and go ahead taking care not to actually touch your eye with the bottle.

8 You develop a skin rash and pains in your joints while taking some prescribed medicine. Do you:

a   Telephone the doctor to report this.

b   Carry on regardless.

c   Stop taking the medicine and hope you get better.

Answers

Safe bets

1	c
2	b
3	b
4	a
5	b
6	c
7	a
8	a
9	b

If you score eight or more you are qualified to look after your own body

Definitely dodgy

2	c
3	a
6	b
7	a
8	c
9	a

Downright dangerous

1	a and b
2	a
3	c
4	b and c
5	a and c
7	b
8	b
9	c

What are the alternatives?

Work in pairs to check out your rights to NHS treatment.

What rights do you have as an NHS patient?

Under the NHS, free treatment is available from a GP, a hospital and community services.

Treatment is also available free to certain people from dentists and opticians. Others receive NHS treatment and pay some of the cost, but not as much as if they were private patients.

Certain people have the right to get free NHS prescriptions, milk and vitamins, NHS wigs and fabric supports and hospital travel costs.

Leaflets with the titles *The Patients' Charter, Help with NHS Costs, Patients' Rights,* available from your local Community Health Council, give you more details about your rights as an NHS patient and what to do if you are not satisfied with your treatment.

Using the leaflets from your local Community Helath Council to see if you can find out whether the following statements are true or false

1 You can change your GP. True/false

2 You have an absolute right to a second opinion. True/false

3 You can say no to being part of medical student training. True/false

4 You should be shown respect for your privacy, dignity and religious and cultural beliefs. True/false

5 You get free prescriptions if you are sixteen or over but under nineteen and still in full-time education. True/false

6 You will find lists of local dentists and GPs in your local library. True/false

7 You can complain about hospital treatment but not about GP treatment. True/false

8 Your health records may be shown to others eg your employer. True/false

ANSWERS - 1: True (Patients' Charter), 2: False (Patients' Charter), 3: True (Patients' Charter), 4: True (Patients' Charter), 5: True (Patients' Charter), 6: True (Patients' Charter), 7: False (Patients' Charter), 8: False (Patients' Charter).

What are the alternatives?

But what if, after a course of treatment from your doctor, you don't seem to be getting any better? Many people (over one in seven of us) have tried alternative or complementary treatments. Some of these are offered by qualified doctors. Others can be offered by people with a non-medical training and others can be offered by people with no training at all who simply decide to put a nameplate up.

Brainstorm the names of complementary treatments you have heard of.

Basic questions

But how could you know if they were worth trying?
Could any do more harm than good?
Are they just an expensive rip-off?
How would you find a good practitioner, if you were interested?
Can you find anyone who has personal experience of such approaches?

There is a selection of research topics available. Working in pairs, volunteer to take a topic. Cover as many as possible in your class. Each pair should produce a presentation on their topic, like those on page 10. Your teacher will give you a time limit.

Research methods you could try include: looking at the information in your *student booklet*, going to the school and local library, looking in the phone book and writing to organisations for information, asking family/friends about personal experiences, checking if practitioners are advertised in local paper.

Methods of presentation might include:

Speech

Article

Question and Answer Session

Taped Report

Poster

Extra credit will be given to those who use local information and sources. (Local Community Health Councils and Yellow Pages are a good source.)

Complementary medicine

Does it work?

The doctors' association, the BMA, says that there is no scientific proof that it works. A Which magazine survey in 1986 found that eighty two per cent of members claimed to have been cured or improved by their treatment. Fifteen per cent said that the treatment was ineffective or made the problem worse. Seventy four per cent said they would definitely use this form of medicine again. Remember that being healthy is about diet, exercise, lifestyle, and positive self-image. Working on the things we can control is likely to make us feel better.

What kinds of things can be treated by complementary medicine?

A Which magazine survey in 1986 found that seventy on per cent of members wanted help with pain or a joint problem. Fifteen per cent of members wanted help with some sort of psychological problem. Most had already sought advice from their GP but were dissatisfied because they had not been cured, had only temporary relief or couldn't be treated. Pain and stress can be long-lasting conditions for which conventional medicine can sometimes do little. On the other hand not many people would consider doing anything else than going to hospital after an accident or emergency.

How can I find out more?

The trouble with complementary medicine is that because it is not part of the NHS it is very difficult to get reliable information about it. People charge fees for it so obviously you need to read their adverts with a 'pinch of salt'.

Another problem is that there is no national system of training and qualifications which covers practitioners of the treatments. Literally anyone can set themselves up as a therapist, sometimes after a weekend course. This means that it is very important to be wary about what you are told and to ask a lot of questions if you are to avoid 'quacks'. Here are some questions you should ask:

- What methods of treatment do you use? What does this involve?
- Where else have you practised?
- Have you successfully treated people for my condition?
- When and where were you trained? How long was the course? Was that full or part-time? What diplomas do you hold?
- How long have you been practising each therapy?
- Could I contact a previous patient of yours to find out what the treatment involves?
- To what professional associations do you belong?
- Does your practice carry a professional indemnity insurance?
- What are your fees?
- Do any of the local doctors refer patients to you?
- Could you give me any literature describing your treatment?

What sorts of things should we report on in our presentation?

Do you believe the claims that are made about the topic you have researched? Do you think it could be worth trying? Could it do more harm than good? Is it just an expensive rip-off? How would you find a good practitioner, if you did go in for one? Is there a register? What address could you write to? How long is the training? Have you found anyone who has personal experience of such approaches? Are there any local practitioners?

Complementary medicine • continued •

Acupuncture

British College of Acupuncture
8 Hunter St, London WC1N 1BN, Tel. 0171 837 6429

British Medical Acupuncture Society
66 - 69 Chancery Lane, London WC2 1AF

The British Acupuncture Association
34 Alderney St, London SW1V 4EU, Tel. 0171 834 1012

Treatment involves inserting needles into acupuncture points or 'meridians'. The needles may be moved while in place or attached to an electric current. Most people who visit an acupuncturist do so for help with pain. In some parts of China it is still used during operations as an anaesthetic. It is also used to help addicts, such as alcoholics, nicotine addicts or heroin addicts, in the belief that it helps deal with withdrawal symptoms like feeling irritable. In traditional Chinese medicine acupuncture is used to treat many illnesses. 'Scientific acupuncture' is used by some Western doctors to ease pain by stimulating the nervous system.

Training is of two kinds – Non-medical provided by a range of colleges for various lengths of time, and Medical which is a course for people who are already qualified as doctors.

Herbalism

National Institute of Medical Herbalists (keeps a register)
56 Longbrook Street, Exeter, Devon EX4 6AH, Tel 01392 426022

General Council and Register of Consultant Herbalists
Marlborough House, Swanpool, Falmouth Cornwall TR11 4HW
Tel. 01326 317321

Treatment involves tinctures of various herbs and plants said to have medicinal properties. (Plants are used to make many drugs. Be careful. Some are known to cause harmful effects if taken in too strong a dose.) Diet, exercise and lifestyle will also be discussed. Many medical herbalists make their own remedies. People visit a herbalist for help with allergies, stress or headaches and other general feelings of being unwell.

Complementary medicine • continued •

Osteopathy

British Naturopathic and Osteopathic Association
Goswell House, 2 Goswell Road, Street, Somerset BA16 0UG, Tel. 01458 840072

College of Osteopaths
6 Netherall Gardens, London NW3 5RR, Tel. 0171 435 6464

The General Council and Register of Osteopaths
Goswell House, 2 Goswell Road, Street, Somerset BA16 0UG, Tel. 01458 840072

Treatment involves observing the way you walk, stand and sit and having your spine examined. Osteopaths use their hands to massage the spine and put the joints through a range of movements. Most people who visit an osteopath do so for help with back pain.

Training is provided by a range of colleges and is usually four years. There is a register of qualified osteopaths (see above).

Homoeopathy

British Homoeopathic Association (keeps a register of medically-qualified homoeopaths) 27a Devonshire St London W1N 1RJ Tel. 0171 935 2163

Society of Homoeopaths (keeps a register of non-medically-qualified homoeopaths. Homoeopaths should have studied for at least 3 years.)
2 Artizan Rd Northampton Northants NN1 4HU Tel. 01604 21400

Treatment involves taking homoeopathic medicines. Like is used to treat like, eg a plant which causes certain symptoms in a healthy person is used to treat those symptoms in an unhealthy person. The patient will be asked to provide full details of his or her symptoms. People visit a homoeopath for help with joint pain, allergies, stress or headaches and other conditions such as chest problems.

Training is of two kinds: Non-medical provided by a range of colleges for various lengths of time, and Medical which is a course for people who are already qualified as doctors. If you go to a GP who is qualified as a homoeopath you can get the treatment free on the NHS.

Complementary medicine • continued •

Naturopathy

British Naturopathic and Osteopathic Association
Goswell House, 2 Goswell Road, Street, Somerset BA16 0UG, Tel. 01458 840072

British Register of Naturopaths
1 Albemarle Rd, The Mount, York YO2 1EN

Treatment involves a 'nature cure'. Naturopathists believe that disease is the result of the build-up in the body of waste materials which have piled up as the result of wrong habits of living. If the right methods are used the body can heal itself. Often the first treatment is changing one's diet, eg by fasting to cleanse the body. This may be followed by massage, wholefood diets, vitamin and mineral therapy, mud packs and possibly joint manipulation. The naturopath then teaches the patient not to rely on overeating, coffee, drugs or smoking.

Reflexology

Association of Reflexologists
27 Old Gloucester St, London WC1N 3XX, 0990 673320

Treatment involves deep foot massage. Reflexologists believe that each organ and muscle of the body is connected to a tiny point on the foot where the energy terminates. By feeling for tender parts in the foot, the therapist can find which parts of the body are causing problems. By massaging parts of the foot, tension and circulation can be improved in specific parts of the body.

Complementary medicine • continued •

Hypnotherapy

Association of Qualified Curative Hypnotherapists
8 Balaclava Rd, Kings Heath, Birmingham, W. Mids B14 7SG, Tel. 0121 441 1775

The British Hypnotherapy Association
1 Wythburn Place, London W1H 5WL, Tel. 0171 723 4443

British College of Hypnotherapy
130 Guilders Rd, Chessington, Surrey KT9 3EA, Tel. 0181 397 3146

Treatment involves using relaxation of the conscious mind to establish the cause of the problem and work on it. Under hypnosis most people are fully aware of what is going on and can remember what took place during it. Many people who visit a hypnotherapist do so for help with weight control and smoking. However it is claimed that it can also bring relief to asthma, panic attacks, migraine, eczema, childbirth and insomnia - all those conditions which may be helped by being more relaxed in one's normal life.

Training is of various kinds: Non-medical training is provided by a range of courses, some long, some short.

Aromatherapy

Association of Tisserand Aromatherapists
65 Church Road, Hove, East Sussex BN3 2BD, Tel. 0273 206640

The International Federation of Aromatherapists
Stanford House, 2-4 Chiswick High Road, London W4 1TH, Tel. 0181 742 2605

Treatment involves using essential oils extracted from plants to rub into the skin of various parts of the body or to inhale. Once on the skin the oil is absorbed fast into the blood stream and it is claimed that different oils can help various disorders, especially those which are stress-related.

Pregnant women should be careful to use only oils from flowers since some others can cause miscarriage.

Training is of various kinds: Non-medical training is provided by a range of courses, some long, some short.

Useful addresses

1   ABC (Anti-Bullying Campaign)
10 Borough High Street
London SE1 9QQ
0171 378 1446
(Factsheet for parents of children who are victims of bullying.)

2   KIDSCAPE
152 Buckingham Palace Road
London
SW1W 9TR
0171 730 3300

(Information on bullying and child protection)

3   TERRENCE HIGGINS TRUST
52-54 Grays Inn Road
London
WC1X 8JU
0171 831 0330

(Leaflets/posters/videos/speakers)

4   ACE (Advisory Centre for Education)
1B Aberdeen Studios
22 Highbury Grove
London N5 2DQ
0171 354 8321

(Useful information sheets on different topics, eg bullying, sex education.)

5   BODY POSITIVE
51b Philbeach Gardens
London
SW5 9EB
0171 835 1045

(Information, leaflets, speakers etc)

6   NATIONAL CHILDBIRTH TRUST
Alexandra House
Oldham Terrace
London
W3 6NH
0181 992 8637

(Provides information and speakers on aspects related to parenthood, birth, feeding and child development.)

7   FAMILY PLANNING ASSOCIATION
27-35 Mortimer Street
London
W1N 7RJ
0171 636 7866

(Leaflets, videos, teaching packs, speakers on relationships, sexuality, abuse, learning difficulties and physical disability)

8   HEALTH EDUCATION AUTHORITY
Marston Book Services
PO Box 87
Oxford
OX2 0DT
01865 204743

(Teaching packs, resources)

9   LESBIAN AND GAY YOUTH MOVEMENT
BM/Gym
London
WC1N 3XX
0171 837 7324

(Teaching packs, resources)

10   BROOK ADVISORY CENTRE
Education and Publications Unit
24 Albert Street
Birmingham
B4 7UD
or
153a East Street
London
SE17 2SP
0171 708 1234

(Large range of resources on sex and personal relationships, unplanned pregnancy and contraception.)

11   DEVELOPMENT EDUCATION CENTRE
Gillet Centre
998 Bristol Road
Birmingham
B29 6LE
0121 472 3255

12 EQUAL OPPORTUNITIES COMMISSION
Overseas House
Quay Street
Manchester
M3 3HN
0161 833 9244

13 DEVELOPMENT EDUCATION PROJECT
801 Wilmslow Road
Didsbury
Manchester
M20 2QR
0161 445 2495

(Particularly good on gender, bullying and race issues.)

14 HEALTH PROMOTION
See under Local Health Authority in phone directory

(A good contact for advice and resources)

15 COMMUNITY HEALTH COUNCIL
As 14

16 CITIZENS ADVICE
As 14

17 CHILDLINE
0800 1111

18 COMMISSION FOR RACIAL EQUALITY
Elliot House
10-12 Allington Street
London
SW1E 5EH
0171 828 7022

19 INSTITUTE FOR THE STUDY FOR DRUG DEPENDANCE (ISDD)
Waterbridge House
32-36 Loman Street
London SE1 0EE
0171 928 1211

20 TACADE
1 Hume Place
The Crescent
Salford
M3 4QA
0161 745 8925

Look at the Help and Support section in useful numbers at the front of your phone book for local contacts.